Desert War

Desert War
The New Conflict Between the U.S. and Iraq

John T. Campbell

Researched by Christine Townsend

New American Library

New American Library
Published by New American Library, a division of
Penguin Putnam Inc., 375 Hudson Street,
New York, New York 10014, U.S.A.
Penguin Books Ltd, 80 Strand,
London WC2R 0RL, England
Penguin Books Australia Ltd, 250 Camberwell Road,
Camberwell, Victoria 3124, Australia
Penguin Books Canada Ltd, 10 Alcorn Avenue,
Toronto, Ontario, Canada M4V 3B2
Penguin Books (N.Z.) Ltd, Cnr Rosedale and Airborne Roads,
Albany, Auckland 1310, New Zealand

Penguin Books Ltd, Registered Offices:
Harmondsworth, Middlesex, England

First published by New American Library, a division of Penguin
Putnam Inc.

First Printing, February 2003
10   9   8   7   6   5   4   3   2   1

 REGISTERED TRADEMARK—MARCA REGISTRADA

LIBRARY OF CONGRESS CATALOGING-IN-PUBLICATION DATA FOR THIS TITLE
IS AVAILABLE UPON REQUEST.

Set in Trade Gothic Light

Printed in the United States of America

PUBLISHER'S NOTE
While the authors have made every effort to provide accurate
telephone numbers and Internet addresses at the time of
publication, neither the publisher nor the authors assume any
responsibility for errors, or for changes that occur after
publication.

BOOKS ARE AVAILABLE AT QUANTITY DISCOUNTS WHEN USED TO PROMOTE
PRODUCTS OR SERVICES. FOR INFORMATION PLEASE WRITE TO PREMIUM
MARKETING DIVISION, PENGUIN PUTNAM INC., 375 HUDSON STREET, NEW
YORK, NEW YORK 10014.

To all allied armed forces who battle
terrorism around the world.

The authors of this book hope that the
differences between the UN and Iraq are
resolved peacefully and none of the
weapons in this book will be used on
anyone.

Contents

Scope

This book was written with the hope of bringing some detail to the public about the upcoming confrontation with Saddam Hussein's Iraq. A brief history of Iraq, a short Saddam Hussein biography, a history of the Persian Gulf War, American motivation, and the Iraqi weapons of mass destruction are discussed in an effort to provide some background and reasons why this conflict is likely to occur.

Attack scenarios are discussed along with the broad strategies of both sides.

Allied forces in the Persian Gulf region are detailed, along with a sampling of American and U.K. air, land, and sea-based weaponry. Some exotic new weapons, such as Blackout bombs, enormous bunker-buster bombs, and the high-tech directed-energy weapons are revealed. Sensors from which the Allies will derive intelligence about Iraq's battlefield situation are detailed. Data on airborne and space-based radars, optical sensors, and signals intercepts are included.

Special Forces of the United States and the U.K. are detailed with short histories, mission profiles, and weapons data. Projected uses in another war with Iraq for these highly trained, tough troops are also given.

Iraqi force details are also listed with estimates of their capability, strengths and weaknesses. A land and seaborne mine warfare section is included as Iraq's possibly only effective weapon against the prodigious forces fielded by the Allies.

The details make it very clear: Iraq will not have a chance against the United States and its allies in another war. However, if Saddam Hussein decides to rain chemical, biological, or nuclear weapons on Allied invasion forces, casualties will mount and the decision to disarm Saddam and remove him from power may be second-guessed.

But this is precisely the point. The idea is to disarm him *before* he acquires enough weapons to inflict massive casualties on invading armies, or on neighboring nations, such as Israel, Iran, Saudi Arabia, or Kuwait.

Introduction

On September 11, 2001, the United States endured the worst terrorist attack in its history. Nineteen terrorists from the al-Qaeda terrorist organization led by Osama bin Laden hijacked four commercial aircraft and drove two of them into the World Trade Center in New York City and one into the Pentagon in northern Virginia. The fourth plane was driven into the ground in Pennsylvania after the passengers fought with the terrorists.

This monstrous incident led to the declaration of war by the United States on terrorists worldwide, and especially on al-Qaeda, bin Laden's organization. The United States swiftly attacked Afghanistan, a nation ruled by the Taliban, who had given the al-Qaeda organization a home in their country. In a matter of months, the Taliban were routed and driven from power, and al-Qaeda was dealt a serious blow.

The George W. Bush administration then turned its attention to a far more dangerous adversary, Iraq, with its megalomaniacal leader, Saddam Hussein. Iraq's drive to acquire weapons of mass destruction and its desire to use them made the Iraq situation immediate and infinitely more dangerous. President George W. Bush announced that the goal of the United States was to effect a regime change in Iraq to a more moderate rule. He also demanded that Iraq abide by existing United Nations resolutions that Iraq destroy all its weapons of mass destruction. The buildup to a second war with Iraq had begun.

Desert War

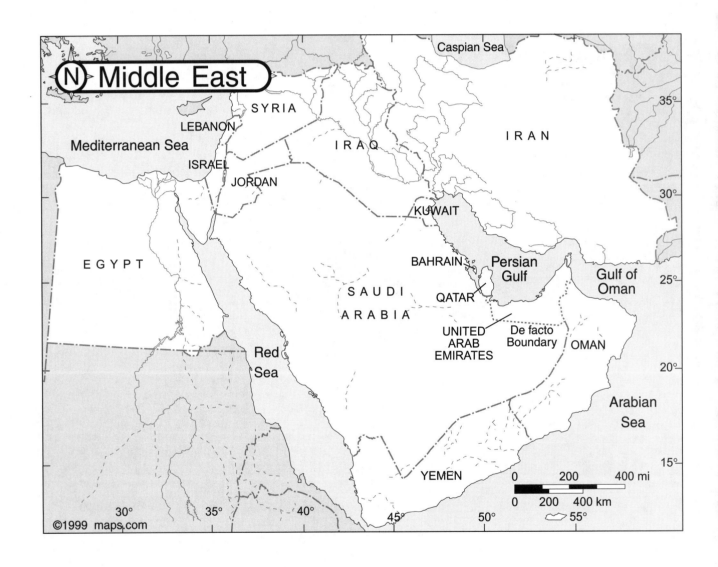

Iraq History

On October 13, 1932, Iraq became a sovereign nation under the leadership of King Faisal and was admitted to the League of Nations, the precursor organization of the United Nations. The new nation encompassed Assyrians, Kurds, Sunnis, Shias, and Iraqi nationalists, who all fought for influence in the new political scene. The stability under King Faisal was lost when he died in 1933. He was succeeded by his inexperienced son, Ghazi, who was unable to find a political balance between national and British pressures under the Anglo-Iraqi alliance then in existence.

In 1939, Ghazi was killed in an auto accident and was succeeded by his infant son with his cousin as regent. In the years before World War II, Iraq rebuffed Nazi approaches and severed diplomatic relations with Germany. Britain reoccupied Iraq after an ultranationalist took power in 1941. In 1943, Iraq declared war on the Axis powers and after the war Iraq joined the United Nations. In 1947, Iraq strongly objected to the partition of Palestine, which allowed the creation of the State of Israel. Iraq supported the Arab side in the Arab-Israeli War of 1948.

The 1950s saw growth in oil production and resulting improvement in revenues. The monarchy was overthrown in 1958, with officers from the army declaring a new republic. Abd al-Karim Qasim, with support from communists, eventually succeeded to power from the group who had seized power from the monarchy. He established close relations with the Soviet Union, and weapons began to flow into Iraq from Russia. After a fight with the Kurds, Qasim cracked down on his own forces, the People's Resistance Force. The Baath Party decided killing Qasim was the only way to eliminate him; Saddam Hussein made the attempt but only injured him. Qasim suppressed the Baath Party as a result, then alienated the communists by purging many from the government. He alienated the West by laying claim to Kuwait. When the Arab League accepted Kuwait as a member, Qasim broke diplomatic relations with his Arab neighbors.

In 1963, Qasim was overthrown, and after some turmoil the Baath Party assumed power. In late 1963, the Baath Party was overthrown by another group of military officers. Abd as Salaam Arif took over, but was killed in a helicopter crash in 1966, his brother taking control for a brief period. Two men, Abd ar Razzaq an Narif and Ibrahim au Daud took control, but the Baath Party wrested power back from them in 1968. Saddam Hussein was a key leader behind the scenes and created the Iraqi secret police to keep track of their political enemies. Saddam Hussein and Hassan al-Bakar dominated the Baath Party and were joined by General Adnan Talfah, Saddam's brother-in-law.

On July 16, 1979, Saddam Hussein became president, secretary-general of the Baath Party Regional Command, and commander in chief of the Iraqi armed forces. On September 23, 1980, after deteriorating relations with Iran over a disputed waterway leading to the Persian Gulf, Iraqi forces invaded Iran.

The brutal Iran-Iraq War, called the Gulf War by those involved (not to be confused with the Persian Gulf War in 1990–1991), began with Iraqi gains and the capture of the disputed waterway, coupled with the retreat of the poorly equipped Iranians. Iran finally stopped the Iraqi forces with human wave attacks. The Iraqis were forced to retreat in early 1982 after Iran used untrained soldiers ranging in age from nine to fifty to run over minefields to clear paths for tanks in a tactic reminiscent of the Soviet Army in World War II. The front lines swept back and forth over the next two years. There was a horrifying report of the Iranians using human wave attacks—thousands of children roped together in groups of about twenty to prevent them from deserting. The human wave attacks had little effect on the strategic situation.

Iraq used chemical weapons on advancing Iranians and missile attacks on Iranian cities. The war wound down in the late 1980s, and the casualty toll was horrific.

Beyond the human toll was the enormous debt incurred by Iraq to fund the war with Iran. This led Saddam Hussein into conflict with his Arab neighbors over the production and price of oil, thus setting the stage for the war over Kuwait, called by Westerners the Persian Gulf War.

Casualties, Iran-Iraq War

	Iraq	Iran
Killed	100,000	250,000
Wounded	150,000	500,000

Saddam Hussein Bio

Born in Tikrit, Iraq, in 1937, Saddam Hussein attended Cairo University in Egypt and Al-Mustansariyah University in Baghdad. He joined the Baath Party in 1956 and became active in the numerous coups and countercoups during that time. After being sentenced to death for the attempted assassination of Iraqi Prime Minister Qasim, he fled Iraq and lived in exile in Egypt and Syria from 1959 to 1963. After returning to Iraq in 1964, he was arrested for plotting to overthrow then-president Abd as Salaam Arif. He played a leading role in the July 1968 revolution. He became a general in Iraq's military in 1976 and assumed the presidency of Iraq in 1979.

He is married to Sajida Khayrallah, who had five children, three daughters and two sons. Saddam has had more than one mistress. One was married when Hussein became infatuated with her. Her husband quickly agreed to give up his wife to Saddam. Saddam's son Uday discovered the affair and murdered Saddam's valet, who had acted as liaison between Saddam and his mistress. Uday was temporarily exiled to Switzerland, then returned to Iraq a few years later. Parisoula Lampsos was another mistress of Hussein, for thirty years. She has since defected and has given personal information to Western intelligence agencies. He is a man of some contradictions. Seemingly kind to children, he has tried to murder one of his own sons, leaving the son paralyzed. He is a fan of Frank Sinatra, and dances to his music. His favorite movie is *The Godfather*. Hussein likes to have alcoholic drinks and smoke cigars as he watches videos of his enemies being tortured. He takes Viagra for sexual prowess, but is reported to have had a stroke. There are persistent reports that he has had doubles created via plastic surgery to stand in for him in case of assassination attempts.

Several attempts have been made to remove Hussein from power since the Persian Gulf War.

An attempt was made on Saddam Hussein's life in 1996 by elements of the Iraqi army, who set off a bomb outside one of his palaces. Hundreds of officers were arrested, including officers from the Republican Guard, and dozens were executed.

His life is riddled with violence and paranoia. He established Iraq's secret police to eliminate political opposition in order to stay in power. Soon after becoming president he invaded Iran, using the excuse that Iran had prevented Iraq's access to the sea; the Iran-Iraq War went on for eight bloody years and killed hundreds of thousands on both sides. He has used chemical weapons on Iranians and on the Kurds, his own people, killing men, women, and children. And in August 1990 he invaded Kuwait, sacking and destroying the country, and precipitating the Persian Gulf War, in which a coalition of forces led by the United States destroyed half his army and killed tens of thousands of Iraqi military personnel. He is said to have cried when the coalition forces thoroughly defeated Iraqi forces.

Hussein is said to have personally shot dead one of his generals over a disagreement. He is suspected to have purged many of the commanders who served during the Persian Gulf War to eliminate them as potential opponents. This harkens back to the Soviet purges of its military by Stalin, who feared the same opposition. He has an enormous ego, common to dictators, but lives in abject fear of assassination.

The closest he came to being killed was during the Persian Gulf War when he drove around Baghdad in any vehicle he could find. Coalition intelligence discovered he was driving around in a Winnebago, so Winnebagoes were targeted. Hussein was in a column of vehicles that was hit by an airstrike. The vehicle in front of him and the vehicle behind him were hit, killing many of his personal bodyguards, but his vehicle was untouched. Hussein seems to have the luck of dictators worldwide. Hitler also survived two assassination attempts by sheer luck.

During the Persian Gulf War, upon hearing that the United States would end the ground war after one hundred hours and not invade the rest of Iraq, he exclaimed, "Then I have won!"

The Persian Gulf War

Saddam Hussein viewed Kuwait as a renegade province, which would ultimately be reunited with Iraq. In 1990, Saddam wanted to increase oil prices and became angry at other Arab states, accusing them of exceeding OPEC-set production quotas, thus driving the price of oil down. He accused these Arab states of shoving a "poisoned dagger" into Iraq's back. In July 1990, Saddam publicly threatened Kuwait and the United Arab Emirates. Other Arab states in the region dismissed his threat because no Arab state had ever attacked another Arab state. This was true even in the case of the Iran-Iraq War: Iraqis are Arabs; Iranians are Aryans. Saddam Hussein also accused Kuwait of stealing $2.5 billion in oil from the Rumaila oil field, which Kuwait and Iraq share.

The Iraqi military had a formidable force at this time. Over 900,000 men in uniform—sixty-three divisions, eight of which were Republican Guards, the Iraqi elite—formed Iraqi armed forces. They were armed with T-72 tanks, South African 155mm heavy artillery, Chinese and Soviet multiple rocket launchers, Chinese Silkworm and French Exocet antiship missiles (a French Exocet hit and severely damaged the USS *Stark*, killing thirty-seven sailors, in a separate prewar incident), MiG-29 and Su-24 fighter aircraft, along with French M1 Mirage aircraft.

An Iraqi military exercise near Basra in southern Iraq suddenly took on an ominous tone as supplies were moved up near troops, and Iraq's army moved toward the Kuwaiti border. The Kuwaiti army at this time numbered only 50,000 men, 245 tanks, 430 armored personnel carriers, 72 artillery pieces, 35 combat aircraft, and 18 armed helicopters. On August 2, 1990, Iraq invaded Kuwait and quickly overwhelmed the outmatched Kuwaitis.

Operation Desert Shield

Within days, the United States offered support to Saudi Arabia, and men and materiel began to flow into the Saudi kingdom. The first U.S. unit sent there was the 82nd Airborne, 4,000 soldiers to help defend Saudi Arabia from attack by the Iraqi army. The relatively lightly armed 82nd would be no match for Iraqi armor, so the U.S. soldiers took to calling themselves "Iraqi speed bumps," a bit of black humor in a desperate situation. The decision had been made at the highest levels of the U.S. government to defend Saudi Arabia from attack. Operation Desert Shield had begun.

A coalition of nations, many of them Arab states, was formed to oppose Iraqi aggression. Joining the United States were the United Kingdom, France, Egypt, Saudi Arabia, Italy, Syria, Qatar, Bahrain, and the United Arab Emirates.

After months of moving enormous quantities of men and equipment into Saudi Arabia, the United States and its coalition allies were ready to go on the offensive.

Operation Desert Storm

A short time later the U.S. government decided to liberate Kuwait and drive Iraq from the country, destroying Iraq's ability to threaten its neighbors.

By mid-January 1991, Iraqi forces were clustered mostly in Kuwait, facing the Saudi border. Coalition forces were grouped along Saudi Arabia's eastern coastline, opposing the Iraqi army.

Air War

The shooting began at 2:40 A.M. on January 16, 1991, when a dozen army and air force Special Operations helicopters streaked into Iraqi airspace, flying in total darkness just thirty feet above the sand to take out two key Iraqi early-warning radar installations on the border. The Iraqi air defense system was patterned on the Soviet systems and was considered to be an effective one by coalition experts. Any air defense system depends upon the quick and reliable transfer of data through the system; therefore the coalition air forces concentrated on the data choke points, the radars and communication nodes in the system, taking them out one by one until Iraqi commanders were blinded to the Allies' moves.

EF-111As, bombers outfitted for electronic warfare, jammed the Iraqi radars, while F4-Gs (Wild Weasels) and F-15Es fired Shrike and HARM antiradiation missiles, which homed in on the Iraqi radars' transmissions and destroyed the radars. Once a path was cleared through the Iraqi air defenses, coalition aircraft barreled through, attacking many targets in the first night. British Tornado fighter-bombers attacked airfields; French and Italian aircraft attacked surface-to-air missile (SAM) sites; U.S. stealth fighters, F-117s, smashed command and control centers and other targets in downtown Baghdad. The Iraqis never saw them coming until it was too late. Tomahawk cruise missiles fired from U.S. Navy warships in the Persian Gulf hit Baghdad's power plants and communications centers.

In two weeks, by the end of January, coalition forces had complete air supremacy. Over the next thirty days, the Iraqi army in Kuwait and elsewhere in Iraq was pounded from the air, with particular attention paid to the Republican Guard. The goals for this air campaign were the suppression of Iraqi air defenses, attrition of enemy ground forces by at least 50 percent, and the support of a ground attack.

Ground War

Ten days before the ground attack began, General H. Norman Schwarzkopf, in a brilliant move, ordered forces deployed westward with the French 6th Light Armored Division at the extreme western end, the 82nd and 101st Airborne Divisions on the French right flank. Next came the bulk of Allied armored strength: the 24th Infantry Division Mechanized, the 3rd Armored Cavalry Regiment, the 1st Armored Division, the 2nd Armored Cavalry Regiment, the 3rd Armored Division, the 1st Infantry Division Mechanized, the British 1st Armoured Division, and the 1st Cavalry Division Armored.

The Iraqi army had two basic options with their tank force: dig in and use their tanks as fixed artillery, or break out and maneuver to duel with Allied armor. If the Iraqis dug in, attempting to camouflage their units to prevent detection by day, the day's brutal sun would heat up the massive metal of each tank, and the tanks would reradiate the heat slowly through the night, allowing A-10 Warthogs and Apache helicopters with formidable tank-killing weaponry to easily detect the tanks, which glowed brightly in the Allies' infrared detectors at night. The Allies, particularly the United States, owned the night and showered Hellfire and TOW missiles on the fixed Iraqis.

If the Iraqi armor maneuvered out in the open, then those same Allied weapon systems would

F-14 Tomcat

US Navy

rain down missiles, bombs from B-52s, and artillery shells during the day and night. So it was dig in, and die, or maneuver, and die. The Iraqis had nowhere to go.

The ground assault into Iraq and Kuwait began on February 23, 1991, with U.S. Marines smashing into Iraqi defenses in Kuwait and the U.S., French, and U.K. armor charging into Iraq in the western end of the battle line. The marines were followed by Arab forces and together they liberated Kuwait. Coalition armor sped across Iraqi desert in a bid to cut off Iraqi forces from escape back into western Iraq. The Republican Guard was targeted for destruction with massed airpower supporting the swift advance of coalition armor toward them.

What followed was the most massive tank battle in history. Coalition forces lost four tanks while destroying over a thousand Iraqi tanks. The reasons for this startling disparity were many. The U.S. M1A1 Abrams tank was vastly superior to even the top-of-the-line Iraqi tank, the T-72, a Soviet model. The M1 had longer range (two miles versus one mile at night), much superior target-

ing, and faster reloading of its main gun. U.S. and Allied tank crews were more highly trained and motivated as well.

After one hundred hours of ground fighting, the United States and its allies decided on a cease-fire. The Republican Guard, although wounded by massive air attacks and pounded by U.S. tanks, escaped to the west with about 60,000 personnel and much of its armor intact. The following figures reflect all air-delivered munitions expended by tactical elements of the USAF, USN, and USMC during the 1991 Persian Gulf War, excluding cannon rounds that may have been fired. These figures do not include missiles fired by U.S. Army helicopters. All costs reflect 1991 U.S. dollars.

Gulf War Casualties

Iraqi casualty estimates vary widely, from 20,000 to 200,000. The U.S. Defense Intelligence Agency estimated after the war that there were roughly 100,000 Iraqi deaths. A number of other

Weapon Type	# Expended	Unit cost	Total cost
Air-to-Air Missiles			
AIM-7M	88	$225,700	$19,861,600
AIM-9M	86	$70, 600	$6,071,600
Total	**174**		**$25,933,200**
Unguided Iron Bombs			
Mk-82 lo-drag (500 lb GP)	69,701	$498	$34,711,098
Mk-82 hi-drag (500 lb GP)	7,952	$1,100	$8,747,200
Mk-83 lo-drag (1000 lb GP)	19,018	$1,000	$19,018,000
Mk-84 lo-drag (2000 lb GP)	9,578	$1,871	$17,920,438
Mk-84 hi-drag (2000 lb GP)	2,611	$2,874	$7,504,014
M-117 lo-drag (750 lb demo)	43,435	$253	$10,989,055
UK-1000 (1000 lb GP)	288	$16,222	$4,671,936
CBU-52/58/71 (frag.)	17,831	$2,159	$38,497,129
CBU-87 (CEM)	10,035	$13,941	$139,897,935
CBU-89 Gator	1,105	$39,963	$44,159,115
Mk-20 Rockeye II	27,937	$3,449	$96,527,163
CBU-72 FAE	254	$3,800	$965,200
CBU-78 Gator	209	$39,963	$8,352,267
Total	**210,004**		**$431,960,550**
Guided Bombs			
GBU-10 (Laser/Mk-84)	2,637	$22,000	$58,014,000
GBU-12 (Laser/Mk-82)	4,493	$9,000	$40,437,000
GBU-15 (EO-IR/Mk-84)	71	$227,600	$16,159,600
GBU-16 (Laser/Mk-83)	219	$150,000	$32,850,000
GBU-24 (LL-laser/Mk-84)	284	$65,000	$18,460,000
GBU-24 (LL-laser/BLU-109)	897	$85,000	$76,245,000
GBU-27 (Laser/BLU-109)	739	$75,539	$55,823,321
GBU-28 (Laser/4000 lb penet.)	2	$100,000	$200,000
Total	**9,342**		**$298,188,921**

Weapon Type	# Expended	Unit cost	Total cost
Anti-Radiation Missiles (ARMS)			
AGM-45 Shrike	78	$89,000	$6,942,000
AGM-88 HARM	1,961	$257,000	$503,977,000
Total	**2,039**		**$510,919,000**
Air-to-Surface Missiles			
AGM-132A Skipper II	12	$31,240	$374,880
AGM-62B Walleye II	133	$70,000	$9,310,000
AGM-65B Maverick (EO)	1,673	$64,100	$107,239,300
AGM-65C Maverick	5	$110,000	$550,000
AGM-65D Maverick (IR)	3,405	$111,000	$377,955,000
AGM-65E Maverick (Laser)	36	$101,000	$3,636,000
AGM-65G Maverick (IR)	177	$269,000	$47,613,000
AGM-84E SLAM	7	$346,000	$2,422,000
Total	**5,448**		**$549,100,160**
Cruise Missiles			
BGM-109 TLAM	298	$1,100,000	$327,800,000
AGM-86C CALCM	35	$1,500,000	$52,500,000
Total	**333**		**$380,300,000**
Helicopter-fired Missiles			
AGM-114 Hellfire (Laser - USN)	30	$35,127	$1,053,810
AGM-114 Hellfire (Laser - USMC)	159	$35,546	$5,651,814
BGM-71 TOW	293	$15,000	$4,395,000
Total	**482**		**$11,100,624**
Grand Total			**$2,207,502,475**

(Source: "Gulf War Air Power Survey," Volume 5)

authoritative estimates put the Iraqi military death toll much lower, at 2,000 to 10,000, with another 2,000 to 5,000 civilian deaths. The numbers are hard to pin down, but they stack up something like this:

Casualties	Coalition	Iraq
Killed Military	U.S. 268	2,000 to
	Allies 77	10,000
Killed Civilians	Kuwait Approx.	2,000 to
	5,000	5,000
POWs	U.S. 45	63,000
	Kuwait 605	
Wounded	Less than 1,000	27,000

Of course this says nothing of what has been called Gulf War syndrome, which has been afflicting U.S. and Allied troops, the cause of which has varied from stress to the depleted uranium from Allied ordnance. Also not shown in the above figures are any Iraqi deaths from the various operations since Desert Storm, or the effect the UN sanctions have had on the Iraqi population.

Equipment Losses

Iraqi equipment losses reflect General Norman Schwarzkopf's orders to his field commanders to inflict maximum losses on Iraqi equipment. He told them to not just bypass equipment in the field, but to destroy it immediately. General Schwarzkopf did not want previously abandoned equipment to come back at the coalition forces hours, or even years, later. The numbers below reflect equipment engaged in the Persian Gulf War. Iraq and obviously the United States have more equipment than that shown in the table.

Equipment	Coalition Forces	Iraqi Forces	Iraqi % losses
Tanks	4 out of 3,360	4,000 out of 4,230	95
Artillery	1 out of 3,633	2,140 out of 3,110	69
APCs	9 out of 4,050	1,856 out of 2,870	65
Helicopters	17 out of 1,959	7 out of 160	4
Aircraft	44 out of 2,600	240 out of 800	30

(Source: www.cryan.com and *Triumph Without Victory* by the *U.S. News & World Report* Staff, Random House, 1992)

War Aftermath to the Present

No-Fly Zones

The northern no-fly zone north of the 36th parallel was established in April 1991 to prevent Iraqi forces from interfering with relief operations to the Kurds. The United States instituted a southern no-fly zone in August 1992, banning all Iraqi aircraft below the 32nd parallel. During Operation Desert Strike, the United States extended the southern no-fly zone to the 33rd parallel. Iraq has periodically attacked coalition aircraft enforcing the no-fly zones with surface-to-air missiles (SAMs). Coalition aircraft have retaliated by attacking radars and SAM sites.

Operation Desert Strike

In 1996, ignoring the warning of the United States, Iraq moved 40,000 troops into northern Iraq to threaten the Kurds, an ethnic group long opposed to Saddam Hussein's rule. President Clinton ordered air strikes on military targets, which were a threat to coalition aircraft over the no-fly zones.

On August 31, 1996, the Iraqi army, led by mechanized Republican Guard troops, captured the Kurdish town of Irbil. Along with this aggression, surface-to-air missiles were launched at coalition aircraft over the no-fly zones.

On September 3, 1996, U.S. cruise missiles struck Iraqi air defense facilities, SAM sites, and command and communications nodes in southern Iraq. USS *Labon* (DDG 58) and USS *Shiloh* (CG 67) launched fourteen cruise missiles, and air force B-52s from Guam launched thirteen conventional air-launched cruise missiles (CALCMs).

On the next day, seventeen Tomahawk cruise missiles were fired from the USS *Russell* (DDG 59), USS *Hewitt* (DD 966), USS *Labon,* and nuclear-powered attack submarine USS *Jefferson City* (SSN 759).

Subsequent deployments of F-117 stealth fighters, F-16 fighter aircraft, a heavy brigade task force, and two U.S. Navy aircraft carriers convinced Iraq to stand down. The southern no-fly zone was expanded from the 32nd parallel to the 33rd parallel, reaching just south of Baghdad. This forced all tactical Iraqi aircraft to more northern bases and thereby reduced the threat to coalition aircraft.

Following Operation Desert Strike, Iraqi forces withdrew to their garrisons.

Operation Desert Fox

On December 16, 1998, President Clinton ordered cruise missile strikes on military targets and weapons of mass destruction facilities in Iraq for Iraq's continued noncompliance with UN resolutions and for interfering with UN Special Commission (UNSCOM) weapons inspectors.

In addition, U.S. and U.K. aircraft launched several hundred sorties and one hundred bombing raids over the seventy-hour campaign. Three hundred Tomahawk cruise missiles were launched along with one hundred air-launched cruise missiles.

Republican Guard positions were pounded by the U.K.'s Royal Air Force (RAF). Over seventy-five targets were struck during Desert Fox, degrading Saddam Hussein's ability to manufacture weapons of mass destruction and his ability to deliver those weapons to his enemies. Iraq's ballistic missile research and production facilities were hit, which was estimated to set back Iraq's missile program by a year. A refinery at Basra was attacked due to its involvement in illegal oil exports.

Iraq's "anthrax air force" was attacked, and its capability significantly degraded. This "anthrax air force" consisted of training planes converted into pilotless aircraft capable of delivering chemical or biological weapons. The planes were L-29s from Czechoslovakia.

During this campaign, the term "degraded" was used quite often. The problem intelligence agencies had was determining how degraded Iraq's capabilities were. Only soldiers on the ground could definitively determine what the damage really was. This may have shaped resolve in 2002 to finally force Saddam Hussein from power and have an unfettered UN inspection of the entire country.

Iraq's Pilotless Program— Saddam's "Anthrax Air Force"

General Characteristics

Configuration: single engine, dual-seat trainer
Size: 35 feet (10.8 meters) long, 10 feet (3.1 meters) high
Range: 837 miles (1350 kilometers)
Speed: 143 miles per hour (231 kilometers per hour) maximum

Flight ceiling: 35,700 feet (10,900 meters)
Potential armament: Two 220-pound (100-kilogram) bombs, or four rockets
CBW potential: 2,000-liter spray tanks; 500-gallon drop tank
Manufacturer: Aero Vodochody of Czechoslovakia
Iraqi complement: Seventy-eight L-29s and ninety L-39s; estimates are that only a fourth of these aircraft are still in service

UN Weapons Inspections

The Iraqi Nuclear Weapons Program

By the early '90s, Iraq had spent billions of dollars and had employed approximately 12,000 people in its quest for nuclear weapons.

The Iraqi nuclear program began in the 1960s when Iraq bought a 2-megawatt light water research reactor from the Soviet Union. Tammuz I, a 50-megawatt French research reactor, was purchased sometime later, but was bombed in 1981 by Israel. This attack prompted the Iraqis to enshroud their nuclear program in secrecy, the details of which came to light only with the UN weapons inspection program after the Persian Gulf War. Iraqi officials provided intermittent cooperation and gradually grew hostile as the inspectors uncovered massive amounts of data documenting the Iraqi drive for nuclear weapons.

Nuclear Weapons Program Locations

Al Tuwaitha—nuclear program research center, location of centrifuge and electromagnetic isotope separation (EMIS) uranium enrichment efforts
Tarmiyah—uranium enrichment; capable of producing 15 kilograms of highly enriched uranium per year, enough for one bomb; bombed during the Persian Gulf War

Ash Sharqat—duplicate facility of Tarmiyah
Akashat—phosphate mine, producing
  "yellowcake," a uranium oxide
Al Qaim—uranium oxide processing plant
Al Furat—centrifuge manufacturing facility
Fallujah—calutron storage site
Al Qa Qaa—manufacturing site for explosive
  "lenses" for an implosive-type nuclear weapon
Al Atheer—weapon parts testing

The basic problem in making a nuclear weapon is fourfold: Enough fissile material has to be acquired to create a nuclear explosion; the material must be separated from other isotopes and purified or enriched; the design must be "weaponized"; and the weapon must be tested.

During the 1980s Iraq acquired 450 metric tons of uranium oxide, called yellowcake. Iraq also mined 164 metric tons of yellowcake. Iraq then needed the means to enrich the uranium to weapons grade.

The "Smoking Gun"—Discovery of Iraqi Calutrons and Gas Centrifuges

One of the first hard evidences of the extent of the Iraqi nuclear weapons program was the discovery of calutrons, which are used in uranium enrichment. Seized documents indicated that ninety of these devices were in Iraqi hands. Calutrons are used in electromagnetic isotope separation, EMIS, to separate U-238 from the highly fissile, and highly sought, U-235.

UN weapons inspectors also found evidence that gas centrifuges had been used by Iraqi nuclear scientists to separate small quantities of the uranium isotopes.

Additional evidence was uncovered which showed that Iraqi scientists knew everything necessary to build a gun-type nuclear device. Iraqi scientists also knew that gun-type nuclear weapons are very difficult to deliver using a missile, so they concentrated on the implosive-type device, which can deliver greater yields and also be delivered by a missile.

After many inspection trips, the UN weapons inspectors were withdrawn from Iraq on December 16, 1998. The United States and its coalition allies pursued a bombing campaign, Operation Desert Fox, attempting to destroy Iraq's capability to produce weapons of mass destruction.

In late 2002, UN weapons inspectors returned for the first time since 1998 with great pressure on them to discover the truth about Iraqi weapons of mass destruction.

Attack Options

In any option for a war with Iraq, Pentagon planners want to engage the Iraqi people in their quest to overthrow Saddam Hussein. They therefore do not want to target civilian infrastructure, such as food sources, power plants, etc. The United States also does not want to engage the Iraqi military in the cities where severe casualties could be inflicted on any invading force. This is borne out by the experience in many wars, such as World War II, when, in one example, the Soviet Army suffered 100,000 casualties taking Berlin from the German army. A recent example, on a much smaller scale for the United States, is the Somalia conflict in which the U.S. Special Forces took many casualties chasing a Somali warlord in the city of Mogadishu. The Iraqis recognize that the United States is very sensitive to casualties, therefore Iraq would be expected to draw U.S. forces into situations where maximum casualties could be inflicted, even if it cost many Iraqi lives. To avoid this, the United States and its allies would encircle cities and wait until Iraqi forces collapse.

One interesting aspect of any operation would be the establishment of air bases inside Iraq's borders, particularly in the western desert near Jordan, where sortie lengths would be very short.

One very large question looms: Would Saddam Hussein, when faced with certain death, resort to chemical or biological weapons to attack an invading army? Saddam had the same option during the Persian Gulf War and opted not to use these weapons for fear of retaliation in kind by coalition forces. But then he still had hope that he could survive the war, which is what happened. In a new confrontation in which his very survival is at stake, his inhibitions against using chemical and biological weapons might disappear.

Outside-In Option

The United States and its allies would invade Iraq from three sides, the north, west, and south. Turkey, Kuwait, Qatar, Bahrain, the United Arab Emirates, and possibly Saudi Arabia would be the staging areas for an invasion, employing overwhelming airpower to gain swift control of the skies over Iraq. With the no-fly zones in place, this would be done rather quickly. Then the ground war would begin, using armor and mechanized units, engaging and destroying Iraqi armor and infantry. This option would be most like the Persian Gulf War. This may require 250,000 troops or more depending upon Iraqi capabilities.

What to Expect

Air War

The U.S. military and its allies would attempt to accomplish essentially the same things that were done in the Persian Gulf War.

- First take out early-warning radars by sending in decoys to get the Iraqi operators to turn on their radar transmitters, then fire antiradiation missiles to destroy the radar.
- Destroy the Iraqi air defense network and create lanes of entry into Iraqi airspace (the United States has control of most of it already over the no-fly zones).
- Plant computer viruses into the air defense network months before to aid in this destruction.
- Send bombers, cruise missiles, and stealth bombers in to destroy command and control facilities all over Iraq. Computer viruses will aid here as well.
- Destroy the Iraqi air force.
- Use directed-energy weapons to destroy electronics at weapons of mass destruction sites around Iraq.
- Destroy land armies, tanks, artillery, vehicles, etc.

Aircraft from four carrier battle groups from the U.S. Sixth Fleet in the Mediterranean and the U.S. Fifth Fleet in the Persian Gulf will attack Iraq, along with cruisers launching Tomahawk cruise missiles.

U.S. Air Force aircraft will attack from the south from existing bases in Saudi Arabia, and from the north from bases in Turkey. Incirlik Air Base near Adana hosts F-15, A-10, and F-16 fighters, plus U.S. Navy EA-6 Prowler electronic warfare aircraft. B-52 bombers will come from Diego Garcia to pound exposed targets, personnel formations, and armor.

B-1 bombers will fly in from an airbase in Oman. Also from Oman will come British elite Special Air Services soldiers, supported by U.S. AC-130 Spectre gunships. From Qatar will come fighter-bomber aircraft, air-to-air refueling aircraft, and JSTARS reconnaissance aircraft. Qatar also hosts Predator and Global Hawk squadrons, which will keep a close eye on the battlefield.

During the Persian Gulf War, the Iraqi air defense was reduced to firing antiaircraft (AAA, or triple-A) guns into the sky at random with no targets in their sites. They had been blinded by the Allies' combination of antiradiation missiles and use of stealth aircraft. The same tactic is expected this time as well, with the Allied air forces pounding lanes through Iraqi triple-A sites to allow safe access to Iraqi targets.

Ground War

Allied armies will try to accomplish the same goals as in the Persian Gulf War with an important exception: Saddam Hussein will no longer be in power at the end of the ground war.

- Send Special Forces to surreptitiously enter Iraq and be the eyes and ears of the coalition forces, bringing "ground truth" intelligence back to the field commanders and the theater commander.
- Attack the Iraqi army on the ground with large armor units, supported with massive air power, to quickly and efficiently destroy Iraq's land army.
- Destroy Iraq's ability to make war on its neighbors by destroying the military infrastructure, its bases, armor, artillery, and weapons of mass destruction.
- Destroy Saddam Hussein's basis of power, the Republican Guard, and Iraqi secret police.

Any coalition of forces led by the United States would try to engage Iraqi armor across the broadest front in the flattest terrain possible. That scenario would bring all of the formidable U.S. weaponry to bear, as well as take advantage of Allied armor's superior range and accuracy. The Iraqis, on the other hand, would want to engage Allied armor across the narrowest front possible. They may achieve this by taking advantage of natural terrain, for example, forcing the Allies along narrow roads, creating natural choke points and bringing superior forces to bear locally on a smaller number of Allied tanks. Iraq may achieve some limited success this way against Allied armor, but this could only be done in a thick overcast, which would limit targeting of Iraqi units by Allied aircraft.

The Iraqis used a classic defensive tank technique during the Persian Gulf War, and they are sure to try to use it again in any upcoming war with a coalition against them. They positioned their tanks on the reverse slopes of wadis, or sand dunes, so that they could fire upward into advancing coalition armor as they came over the crests of the hills. This would have allowed them to fire at the vulnerable undersides of coalition tanks. The tactic did not work in the Persian Gulf War because the Iraqis didn't know that the American tanks were approaching—their reconnaissance vehicles had been destroyed earlier in the day. The U.S. tanks were over the crests of the hills and upon them before the Iraqis knew it.

The danger to Allied armor and infantry in large formations on flat, wide-open terrain is that the Iraqis may use those areas as chemical or bio weapons areas and dump massive quantities of these weapons of mass destruction into the battlefield without hurting their own military or civilian population. These same thoughts ran through the minds of General Norman Schwarzkopf and his staff when faced with the wide-open desert west of Kuwait just before the ground war started in 1991. In his autobiography, *It Doesn't Take a Hero*, Schwarzkopf said Intelligence suggested that the Iraqis may have wanted to "pop a nuke out there." They nicknamed the sector "the chemical killing sack." Analysis after the Persian Gulf War concluded that Saddam Hussein did not use chemical or biological weapons during the war for fear that the United States would retaliate in kind.

Special Operations forces will enter Iraq from Jordan and Djibouti to disrupt Iraqi communications and take out sites that cannot be destroyed from the air. They also can be expected to search for mobile SCUD launchers, which were the nemesis of coalition forces in the Persian Gulf War.

The main ground assault will come from Kuwait and Saudi Arabia by many U.S. units, along with a large British armored division. This time these forces will drive for Baghdad rather than avoid it, but then surround the city rather than fight their way through the narrow streets and alleyways. Any Iraqi units outside the cities will be attacked, but Allied forces will not enter the urban areas and take large numbers of casualties to control every house and street corner. History is replete with examples of armies caught up in house-to-house fighting and enduring many casualties as a result. Germany lost an entire army attacking Stalingrad during World War II.

Allied forces also desperately want to avoid civilian casualties, so as not to appear to crush the people of Iraq. On the other hand, the Allies *do* want to crush Saddam's forces to show the Iraqis that he has lost his iron, totalitarian grip on the nation.

In the Gulf

Bahrain is the home base for Task Force 50, a force of frigates, submarines, and destroyers that patrols the Persian Gulf, intercepting shipping and enforcing UN sanctions against Iraq. Also operating out of Bahrain are surveillance aircraft and a U.S. Navy SEAL unit, along with mine countermeasures ships to prevent any floating or moored mines from hitting naval forces in the Gulf. Some ships were hit by mines during the Persian Gulf War, creating damage and casualties. The meager Iraqi navy will be destroyed in the first few days by aircraft and possibly by Australian or British Special Boat Service forces, along with U.S. Navy SEALs.

Any resupply of Saddam's forces through the Gulf will be stopped by these naval forces.

Inside-Out Option

Up to 80,000 U.S. and Allied Special Forces would be inserted into Iraq by parachute drop, low-level aircraft, and helicopters. They would fight from within the country, using massive Allied air support to bring down the Hussein regime. CIA and Special Forces would seek out and destroy military targets and facilities for Iraq's weapons of mass destruction.

U.S. Special Forces will work with dissident Iraqis, especially the Kurds in the north, to train them, supply them, and support them as they attack the Iraqi military. This is the model for warfare used successfully in Afghanistan. However, the same model was used in Vietnam, but with the opposite result.

"Gulf War Lite"

This operation would be a mix of conventional heavy forces penetrating from outside Iraq and Special Forces attacking from within. This would be an Afghan war scenario but with the armored invasion as well.

Allies Against Iraq

United States

U.S. Central Command— CENTCOM

The headquarters for the overall U.S. effort for Iraq and most of the rest of the Middle East is the U.S. Central Command at MacDill Air Force Base, near Tampa, Florida. The Central Command, or CENTCOM, commanded by Army General Tommy R. Franks, is divided into five service component commands. As war draws near, CENTCOM headquarters will likely shift to the Persian Gulf area, perhaps in Saudi Arabia or Kuwait.

Army Forces Central Command, commanded by Lieutenant General David D. McKiernan, is located at Camp Doha in Kuwait. At this time there are several hundred U.S. tanks and armored personnel vehicles there, along with perhaps 10,000 troops. Joining them is the British 1st Armoured Division of approximately 20,000 personnel.

Naval Forces Central Command is headed by Vice Admiral Timothy Keating, whose headquarters are in Bahrain. This command also serves as the U.S. Fifth Fleet. It controls all U.S. and coalition naval forces supporting operations in Afghanistan and in the Gulf region. Vice Admiral Keating serves as Coalition Force Maritime Component Commander, with a British Royal Marine, Major General Robert Fry, as his deputy. Currently there are eighteen U.S. ships in the Fifth Fleet in three groups, a carrier battle group, an amphibious group, and a task force to intercept shipping. There are many more to come. Another carrier battle group will be added before hostilities are started with Iraq.

Marine Forces Central Command is also located in Bahrain, commanded by Lieutenant General Earl B. Hailston. The USMC 11th Marine Expeditionary Unit has moved into Kuwait.

Central Command Air Forces, headed by Lieutenant General T. Michael Moseley, is headquartered at Prince Sultan Air Base near Al Kharj, about fifty miles south of Riyadh, Saudi Arabia, and controls all U.S. and other coalition air forces in the region. The 363rd Air Expeditionary Wing involved in Operation Southern Watch is based there and oversees flights into the southern Iraq no-fly zone.

Special Operations Command, Central Command (SOCCENT) is Central Command's Special Operations command. Task Force K-Bar, or Combined Joint Special Operations Task

Force–South, is an Allied Special Forces group with U.S. Navy SEALs at its core. Task Force 11, or Task Force Sword, is a force comprised of U.S. Delta Force and Naval Special Warfare Development Group SEAL personnel, along with U.K. Special Air Service troops tasked with pursuing high-value targets.

(Source: The Center for Defense Information, on-line)

United Kingdom and Australia

The U.K. has provided significant support by sending one of their armored divisions, Special Air Service troops, and Tornado fighter aircraft.

Australia is providing maritime reconnaissance aircraft and Special Air Service forces.

New Allied Weapons

Storm Shadow

Britain's contribution to the cruise missile arena is the Storm Shadow, which is entering service with the Royal Air Force. Storm Shadow is an air-launched, conventionally armed, long-range, stand-off, precision weapon, which is deployable in day or night, in most weather and operational conditions.

General Characteristics

Primary function: Destroy sensitive and highly protected targets (command bunkers, communications centers, etc.) with great accuracy

Contractor: Matra BAe Dynamics (MBD)

Weight: 2,800 pounds (1300 kilograms)

Length: 16 feet (5 meters)

Diameter: over 3 feet (1 meter); with wings deployed, less than 10 feet (3 meters)

Range: 155 miles (250 kilometers)

Guidance: TERPROM (TERrain PROfile Matching) terrain navigation with an integrated GPS

Terminal guidance: imaging infrared sensor and autonomous target recognition system

Platforms: Tornado GR4/4A, Harrier GR7/T10, and Eurofighter

Directed-Energy Weapons

Directed-energy weapons fall into the following categories:

- Lasers
- High-powered microwave (HPM) to destroy electronics
- High-powered microwave to inflict pain on personnel
- Plasma weapons—similar to a bolt of lightning

Lasers

Laser weapons are not just for strategic missile defense. The U.S. military is actively working on laser weapons that could be mounted on the new F-35 aircraft or the venerable AC-130 Spectre gunship to complement its cannons and howitzer. Laser types include solid-state lasers, chemical lasers with electro-regeneration of chemicals, and fiber lasers. Lasers work by locally heating a target, melting its way through the outer skin, and possibly detonating fuel tanks or ordnance within the targets. The targets would include ground vehicles, cruise missiles, and air defense sites.

The power required is estimated at 100 kilowatts and could be obtained directly from the aircraft's engine. This would allow engagement of targets at up to six miles. The laser weapons would likely be mounted on a turret arrangement to allow for rapid retargeting of multiple threats.

These weapons are still in development, but the military could take a working prototype and use it against Iraqi targets.

High-Powered Microwave (HPM)

Close to operation is a U.S.-funded, British-designed, directed-energy weapon that would produce a broadband electromagnetic pulse (EMP), which would destroy, disable, reboot, or shut down Iraqi computers. This sort of weapon would fit into the overall strategy of minimizing Iraqi casualties to bring about an uprising of the Iraqi people against Saddam Hussein. A target for a directed-energy weapon might be a communications node manned by civilians. The energy in the pulse wipes out computers and associated electronic equipment but leaves the people unharmed. Deeply buried command and control facilities may also be targets for weapons of this type. Rather than go after a buried target with bunker-busting bombs, which may or may not work, an EMP weapon would destroy the bunker's effectiveness. The pulse would be conducted underground by any telephone wires, power lines, metal structures, coaxial cables, waveguides, and antennas connected to the bunker. Any electronics connected to these lines would be destroyed.

Of course, anything electronic is susceptible to high voltage induced by an electromagnetic pulse. Radars, communications stations, and power plants can be disabled by EMP. This was a concern during the Cold War with the Soviet Union. A nuclear burst at about one hundred miles up would have caused very large EMP, enough to destroy the aforementioned equipment, and also car ignitions, cell phones, TVs, and radios. While a nuclear-generated EMP is not envisioned for use over Iraq due to the enormous political problems in using any nuclear weapon, even in a nonlethal mode, EMP, which is narrowly

focused and directed at a specific target, may be used.

These weapons would be packaged in miniature boxes, which could be easily fitted to cruise missiles, UAVs, or pods dropped from aircraft. They could also go into artillery shells, mines, and one-ton bombs. These weapons are still under development, but an engineering model could be used to take out a specific target.

These weapons fall into two broad categories of implementation, single use and reusable. EMP can be generated by creating a large static electric field, then collapsing it quickly through the use of explosives. The collapsing field creates a large radiating EMP. The other kind is a reusable EMP device, which may be placed on aircraft, or on expendable vehicles, such as a cruise missile, which would fly over multiple targets, then potentially land somewhere for recovery. Up to 100,000 pulses could be radiated into targets on one sortie. Assuming 1,000 pulses per target, 100 targets could be electromagnetically attacked.

A microwave source weighing less than 45 pounds is capable of radiating 1 gigawatt of power within a few nanoseconds. A 400-pound system can radiate 20 gigawatts. In comparison, Hoover Dam generates 2 gigawatts per day. The weapon's electrical generators would be powered by the air vehicle's engines. The pulse would be radiated by a phased array antenna, which is pointed electronically, rather than having to steer a dish toward the target. This allows much faster engagement of targets as the vehicle passes overhead.

One of the more surprising developments is that Iraqi oil sites and weapons of mass destruction storage sites may be taken off the bombing list. The reason is that the economy of Iraq will need oil sales to recover from yet another war with the United States and its allies. Also, the specter of bombed sites issuing chemical and biological material for many days, maybe months, is haunting. These agents may drift into neighboring countries and cause innocent deaths. The United States also does not want to contaminate Iraq or any other country with nuclear isotopes, which take tens of thousands of years to decay to safe levels. Oil and WMD (weapons of mass destruction) sites have become targets for directed-energy weapons. Blow out the electronic and computer infrastructure at these sites and they will be ineffective. Oil will not be pumped, and nuclear, chemical, and biological development and production will cease.

Mobile Pain Ray

This weapon would be mounted on a Humvee and would swivel to "spray" advancing troops or civilians with short pulses of electromagnetic energy at 95 gigahertz. This works by heating skin to very hot temperatures and is akin to having drops of scalding water fall on the skin. This would work even through clothing. The pain stops immediately after leaving the electromagnetic field, and people would naturally seek to escape the field to stop the pain. This is slated for use in urban environments where many noncombatants would be found. No permanent damage is done to skin or internal organs because the field only penetrates one-sixty-fourth of an inch.

Plasma Weapons

These weapons can cause much more physical damage than other types of directed-energy weapons.

There are two possible implementations. One is to create the plasma in a chamber, excite it, introduce a laser-critical gas such as argon, and direct the resultant energy through high-power optics as a laser beam. The other is to wrap small compact rings or toroids of plasma energy in intense magnetic fields and fire them from a weapon as "bullets" at air or ground targets.

The critical technology in this area is creating and storing enormous energy, then releasing it very quickly. A capacitor is an electrical device that stores electrical energy on metal plates sandwiched between a material called a dielectric. A fast capacitor bank called Shiva Star that stores 10 million joules (about 3 kilowatt-hours or 10,000

kilowatt-seconds) of energy and releases it in a fraction of a second has been developed.

These weapons are most probably still in development, but the military could take a working prototype and use it against Iraqi targets.

Information Warfare

During the Persian Gulf War, U.S. intelligence agents planted a computer virus in the Iraqi air defense network's computer system. Computer chips with a National Security Agency–created virus were slipped into a French-made printer, which ultimately was installed inside a command bunker within the Iraqi air defense network. The virus attacked the air defense network's mainframe computers by turning off any computer windows Iraqi console operators opened to access air defense data. The virus worked as planned, but in retrospect it probably was not needed due to the efficient destruction of Iraqi air defenses by the coalition military. Any U.S.-led alliance against Iraq would want to do this again in the upcoming confrontation.

The Allies could attack Iraqi computer networks using the following:

- Computer virus—a program that attaches itself to another program and attacks other software or makes copies of itself to fill up a computer's hard drive. Viruses also can be made to delete files critical to the computer's operation. Some of the more insidious viruses attack a computer's virus-killing software.
- Worm—a program that winds its way through either the computer's memory or a disk and alters data that it accesses. It is different from a computer virus since it does not require a host program.
- Trojan (horse)—a destructive program that disguises itself as an innocent program, but whose real purpose is to destroy computer operation.
- Logic/Time Bomb—a program that is set into operation at a specific time (time bomb) or

after certain program circumstances are met (logic bomb). This would be an attractive method to U.S. agents. The Iraqi air defense network could be programmed to go down just before a coalition air assault began.

Any of these programs could be transferred via e-mail by attaching itself to address lists, or via any data transfer between computers.

One other information-warfare method might be tried, data spoofing. This requires data to be intercepted in its travel from one computer to another, and other data substituted in its place. This would be much harder to do than unleashing viruses and would require a detailed knowledge of the data to be spoofed. One example of data spoofing would be data from a radar site showing advancing coalition aircraft being intercepted, and data showing no targets substituted in its place. Iraqi command centers would show the sector to be clear of coalition aircraft when actually an Allied attack is on its way.

Air Power

B-1 Bomber—Lancer

The B-1 is part of the U.S. military's long-range bomber force, providing massive and rapid delivery of multiple types of weapons against adversaries anywhere around the globe.

This aircraft was originally conceived to penetrate Soviet airspace at Mach 1 and at very low altitudes, fifty to one hundred feet, to enter under Soviet radar coverage and deliver nuclear warheads on Soviet targets. The designers never met the speed and altitude goals and, as with many development programs, costs grew until the B-1 was canceled by the Carter administration. President Reagan resurrected the B-1, and the program began anew.

This aircraft was not in the Persian Gulf during the Persian Gulf War due to problems with avionics and the crash of a test flight. It made its first appearance in combat during Operation Desert Fox in 1998 over Iraq, flying two sorties and dropping 500-pound bombs on Iraqi targets. In 1999, during Operation Allied Force over Kosovo, the B-1 program found new life with seven B-1s dropping 45 percent of the total tonnage dropped by NATO (over 2.5 million pounds of munitions) in one hundred combat missions. Then, during the Afghan War in 2001–2002, B-1s flew many sorties against Taliban targets, dropping CBU-87s and 500-pound bombs. Unfortunately a B-1 bomber crashed in the Indian Ocean near Diego Garcia in December 2001 during the war in Afghanistan.

The plane's critics are strident, claiming that the only success it has had is over defenseless (in an air defense sense) countries, Kosovo and Afghanistan. B-1 proponents claim that it has found a new mission.

Thirty-three of the remaining ninety-three aircraft are slated to be retired to save money.

General Characteristics

Primary function: Long-range, multirole, heavy bomber

Builder: Boeing, North America (formerly Rockwell International, North American Aircraft)

Operations air frame and integration: Offensive avionics, Boeing Military Airplane; defensive avionics, AIL Division

Power plant: Four General Electric F-101-GE-102 turbofan engines with afterburners

Thrust: 30,000-plus pounds with afterburner, per engine

Length: 146 feet (44.5 meters)

Wingspan: 137 feet (41.8 meters) extended forward, 79 feet (24.1 meters) swept aft

Height: 34 feet (10.4 meters)

Weight: Empty, approximately 190,000 pounds (86,183 kilograms)

Maximum takeoff weight: 477,000 pounds (216,634 kilograms)

Speed: 900-plus mph (1,450 km/h; Mach 1.2 at sea level)

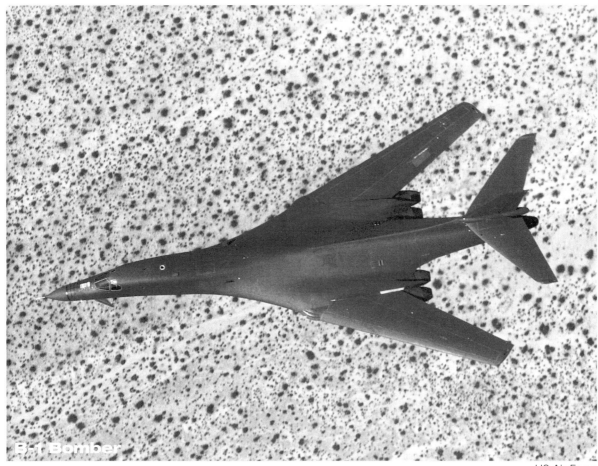

B-1 Bomber

US Air Force

Range: Intercontinental, unrefueled

Ceiling: More than 30,000 feet (9,144 meters)

Crew: Four (aircraft commander, copilot, offensive systems officer, and defensive systems officer)

Armament: Three internal weapons bays can accommodate up to eighty-four Mk-82 general-purpose bombs or Mk-62 naval mines, thirty CBU-87/89 cluster munitions or CBU-97 sensor-fused weapons, and up to twenty-four GBU-31 JDAM GPS-guided bombs or Mk-84 general-purpose bombs

Date deployed: June 1985

Unit cost: $283.1 million (fiscal 1998 constant dollars)

Inventory: Active force, 72; ANG (Air National Guard), 18; Reserve, 0

(Source: USAF Fact Sheets online)

B-2 Bomber—Spirit

The B-2 Spirit is part of the U.S. bomber fleet capable of delivering multiple types of munitions. The B-2 bomber's shape is reminiscent of the air force's Flying Wing, which was designed and built in the 1950s. Designed for stealth, its radar cross section is only a fraction of any other bomber in the U.S. Air Force or in any air force around the world.

This aircraft uses state-of-the-art technology in the form of a special radio-frequency-absorbent coating, a stealth shape, devices to hide heat signatures, and shields to hide aircraft engine turbine blades, to tremendously reduce the radar return from the aircraft. This gives enemy radars no warning as the B-2 approaches. When the aircraft is detected, it is too late for any meaningful defense. It

B-2 Bomber

US Air Force

is most stealthy when radar-illuminated on its front or trailing edge. The aircraft loses some of its stealth when viewed from above or below. However, since Iraq cannot mount any serious fighter aircraft challenge to Allied air power, this will not be a factor in any war with Iraq.

The B-2 is touted by its supporters as a modern bomber using the latest technology. Its detractors, many of them B-1 bomber supporters, call the B-2 too expensive at over $1 billion per aircraft.

General Characteristics

Primary function: Multirole heavy bomber
Prime contractor: Northrop Grumman Corp.
Contractor team: Boeing Military Airplanes

Co., General Electric Aircraft Engine Group, and Hughes Training Inc., Link Division
Power plant: Four General Electric F-118-GE-100 engines
Thrust: 17,300 pounds each engine
Length: 69 feet (20.9 meters)
Height: 17 feet (5.1 meters)
Wingspan: 172 feet (52.12 meters)
Speed: High subsonic
Ceiling: 50,000 feet (15,240 meters)
Takeoff weight (typical): 336,500 pounds (152,635 kilograms)
Range: Intercontinental, unrefueled
Armament: Conventional or nuclear weapons
Payload: 40,000 pounds (18,144 kilograms)
Crew: Two pilots

B-52 Bomber

Unit cost: Approximately $1.157 billion (fiscal 1998 constant dollars)

Date deployed: December 1993

Inventory: Active force, 21 (1 test); ANG, 0; Reserve, 0

(Source: USAF Fact Sheets online)

B-52 Bomber

The B-52 has provided the bulk of the long-range, heavy bomber missions for the last five decades and through all U.S. wars since Vietnam. The bomber is capable of flying at altitudes up to 50,000 feet (15,240 meters). It can carry nuclear or precision-guided conventional ordnance and has been upgraded to provide precision navigation capability.

This venerable aircraft has been around since the 1950s and has been upgraded many times. Originally designed for high-altitude bombing runs over the Soviet Union, the B-52 has been adapted to multiple roles in the conflicts and wars over the last fifty years. Its airframe is obsolete in the stealth age, but the aircraft has contributed by being adapted to carry many different types of ordnance, from dumb iron bombs to sophisticated cruise missiles.

General Characteristics

Primary function: Heavy bomber

Contractor: Boeing Military Airplane Co.

Power plant: Eight Pratt & Whitney engines TF33-P-3/103 turbofan

Thrust: Each engine up to 17,000 pounds

Length: 159 feet, 4 inches (48.5 meters)

A view inside the cockpit of a B-52

Height: 40 feet, 8 inches (12.4 meters)

Wingspan: 185 feet (56.4 meters)

Speed: 650 mph (Mach 0.86; 1,048 km/h)

Ceiling: 50,000 feet (15,240 meters)

Weight: Approximately 185,000 pounds empty (83,250 kilograms)

Maximum takeoff weight: 488,000 pounds (219,600 kilograms)

Range: Unrefueled 8,800 miles (7,652 nautical miles; 14,190 kilometers)

Armament: Approximately 70,000 pounds (31,500 kilograms) mixed ordnance—bombs, mines, and missiles. (Modified to carry air-launched cruise missiles, Harpoon antiship, and Have Nap missiles.)

Crew: Five (aircraft commander, pilot, radar navigator, navigator, and electronic warfare officer)

Accommodations: Six ejection seats

Unit cost: $53.4 million (fiscal 1998 constant dollars)

Date deployed: February 1955

Inventory: Active force, 85; ANG, 0; Reserve, 9

(Source: USAF Fact Sheets online)

F-117A Stealth Fighter— Nighthawk

The F-117A Nighthawk is the world's first operational aircraft designed to exploit radar low-observable stealth technology. Originally conceived as a fighter, the Nighthawk was adapted to carry out attack missions. This precision-strike aircraft penetrates actively defended airspace and uses laser-guided weapons against critical targets.

First used in combat during the Persian Gulf War, the Nighthawk proved its worth delivering ordnance in sortie after sortie on Iraqi targets. The Nighthawk was slated for missions where Iraqi air defenses were still active, and putting its stealth technology to maximum use, the aircraft delivered laser-guided bombs on SAM sites, air defense

F-117

radars, antiaircraft emplacements, and heavily defended command and control bunkers.

General Characteristics

Primary function: Fighter/attack
Contractor: Lockheed Aeronautical Systems Co.
Power plant: Two General Electric F404 non-afterburning engines
Length: 63 feet, 9 inches (19.4 meters)
Height: 12 feet, 9.5 inches (3.9 meters)
Weight: 52,500 pounds (23,625 kilograms)
Wingspan: 43 feet, 4 inches (13.2 meters)
Speed: High subsonic
Range: Unlimited with air refueling
Armament: Internal weapons carriage
Unit cost: $45 million
Crew: One
Date Deployed: 1982
Inventory: Active force, 55; ANG, 0; Reserve, 0
(Source: USAF Fact Sheets online)

F-14 Fighter Aircraft—Tomcat

The F-14 Tomcat is a supersonic, twin-engine, two-seat strike fighter. It has variable sweep-wing geometry to provide the best handling characteristics for air-to-air combat, along with the best carrier landing characteristics. The Tomcat's primary missions are air superiority, fleet air defense, and precision strike against ground targets. This now aging aircraft has provided second-to-none air defense of carrier battle groups around the world. To counter the perceived threat of the Mach 3 MiG-25, the F-14 was outfitted with the one-hundred-mile-range Phoenix missile. The MiG-25 threat was overblown due to its limited combat radius, but the F-14/Phoenix remains unexcelled in long-range, high-altitude intercept capability.

General Characteristics

Function: Carrier-based multirole strike fighter
Contractor: Grumman Aerospace Corporation
Unit cost: $38 million
Propulsion:
F-14A: Two Pratt & Whitney TF-30P-414A turbofan engines with afterburners;
F-14B and F-14D: Two General Electric F110-GE-400 turbofan engines with afterburners

F-14

Thrust:

TF-30P-414A: 20,900 pounds static thrust per engine;

F110-GE-400: 27,000 pounds static thrust per engine

Length: 61 feet, 9 inches (18.6 meters)

Height: 16 feet (4.8 meters)

Maximum takeoff weight: 72,900 pounds (32,805 kilograms)

Wingspan: 64 feet (19 meters) unswept; 38 feet (11.4 meters) swept

Ceiling: Above 50,000 feet (15,240 meters)

Speed: Mach 2-plus

Crew: Two: pilot and radar intercept officer

Armament: Up to 13,000 pounds (5,900 kilograms), to include AIM-54 Phoenix missile, AIM-7 Sparrow missile, AIM-9 Sidewinder missile, air-to-ground precision, strike ordnance, and one M61A1/A2 Vulcan 20mm cannon.

Date deployed: First flight: December 1970

(Source: U.S. Navy Fact File online)

F-15E Fighter Aircraft— Strike Eagle

The F-15E Strike Eagle is a fixed-wing (as opposed to the F-14's swing-wing design), single-seat fighter. The Strike Eagle can perform air-to-air and air-to-ground missions. An array of avionics and electronics systems gives the F-15E the capability to fight at low altitude, day or night, and in inclement weather, and perform its primary function as an air-to-ground attack aircraft.

General Characteristics

Primary function: Air-to-ground attack aircraft

Builder: McDonnell Douglas Corp.

Power plant: Two Pratt & Whitney F100-PW-220 or 229 turbofan engines with afterburners

Thrust: 25,000–29,000 pounds each engine

Wingspan: 42.8 feet (13 meters)

F-15

Length: 63.8 feet (19.44 meters)

Height: 18.5 feet (5.6 meters)

Speed: Mach 2.5-plus

Maximum takeoff weight: 81,000 pounds (36,450 kilograms)

Service ceiling: 50,000 feet (15,240 meters)

Combat ceiling: 35,000 feet (10,670 meters)

Range: 2,400 miles (3,840 kilometers) ferry range with conformal fuel tanks and three external fuel tanks

Armament: One 20mm multibarrel gun mounted internally with 500 rounds of ammunition. Four AIM-7F/M Sparrow missiles and four AIM-9L/M Sidewinder missiles, or eight AIM-120 AMRAAM missiles. Any air-to-surface weapon in the air force inventory (nuclear and conventional)

Crew: Pilot and weapon systems officer

Unit cost: $31.1 million (fiscal 1998 constant dollars)

Date deployed: April 1988

Inventory: Active force, 217; ANG, 0; Reserve, 0

(Source: USAF Fact Sheets online)

F-16 Fighter Aircraft— Fighting Falcon

The F-16 Fighting Falcon is a relatively low-cost, high-performance fighter aircraft for the United States and allied nations. It is highly maneuverable due to its ability to handle high g loads and has proven itself in air-to-air and air-to-ground combat. Being cost effective and highly capable, the Falcon has been exported to many nations around the globe.

In an air combat role, the F-16's maneuverability and combat radius is unexcelled compared to all other potential enemy fighter aircraft. It has all-weather capability and has look-down, shoot-down capability with its ability to detect low-flying aircraft in radar ground clutter.

The F-16 has all-weather capability in an air-to-ground role as well, which allows it to accurately deliver munitions during limited visibility conditions.

Pilots can put up to nine g's—nine times the force of gravity—on the F-16, which exceeds the capability of all other fighter aircraft. This capabil-

F-16

US Air Force

ity generally exceeds the ability of the pilot to withstand g forces, but the aircraft is capable of tighter turns, allowing the pilot to bring his guns or missiles to bear on an opponent in a dogfight.

General Characteristics

Primary function: Multirole fighter
Builder: Lockheed Martin Corp.
Power plant: F-16C/D, one Pratt & Whitney F100-PW-200/220/229 or General Electric F110-GE-100/129
Thrust: F-16C/D, 27,000 pounds
Length: 49 feet, 5 inches (14.8 meters)
Height: 16 feet (4.8 meters)
Wingspan: 32 feet, 8 inches (9.8 meters)
Speed: 1,500 mph (Mach 2 at altitude; 2,420 km/h)
Ceiling: Above 50,000 feet (15,240 meters)
Maximum takeoff weight: 37,500 pounds (16,875 kilograms)
Range: More than 2,000 miles ferry range (1,740 nautical miles; 3,225 kilometers)

Armament: One M61A1 20mm multibarrel cannon with 500 rounds; external stations can carry up to six air-to-air missiles, conventional air-to-air and air-to-surface munitions, and electronic countermeasure pods
Unit cost: F-16A/B, $14.6 million (fiscal 1998 constant dollars); F-16C/D, $18.8 million (fiscal 1998 constant dollars)
Crew: F-16C, one; F-16D, one or two
Date deployed: January 1979
(Source: USAF Fact Sheets online)

F/A-18 Fighter/Attack Aircraft—Hornet

The Hornet is the U.S. Navy's single-seat, fixed-wing, all-weather fighter and attack aircraft. It was designed for traditional strike applications such as close air support for ground forces and supply interdiction while simultaneously keeping its fighter capabilities. With its excellent fighter and self-defense capabilities, the F/A-18 also performs fleet defense missions.

F-18

General Characteristics, C and D Models

Primary function: Multirole attack and fighter aircraft

Contractor: Prime: McDonnell Douglas; Major subcontractor: Northrop

Unit cost: $29 million

Propulsion: Two F404-GE-402 enhanced-performance turbofan engines

Thrust: 17,700 pounds static thrust per engine

Length: 56 feet (16.8 meters)

Height: 15 feet, 4 inches (4.6 meters)

Maximum takeoff gross weight: 51,900 pounds (23,537 kilograms)

Wingspan: 40 feet, 5 inches (13.5 meters)

Range:

Combat: 1,089 nautical miles (1,252.4 miles; 2,003 kilometers), clean plus two AIM-9s;

Ferry: 1,546 nautical miles (1,777.9 miles; 2,844 kilometers), two AIM-9s plus three 330-gallon tanks

Ceiling: 50,000-plus feet (15,240-plus meters)

Speed: Mach 1.7-plus

Crew:

A, C, and E models: One;

B, D, and F models: Two

Armament: One M61A1/A2 Vulcan 20mm cannon

External payload: AIM-9 Sidewinder, AIM-7 Sparrow, AIM-120 AMRAAM, Harpoon, HARM, SLAM, SLAM-ER, Maverick missiles; Joint Stand-Off Weapon (JSOW); Joint Direct Attack Munition (JDAM); various general-purpose bombs, mines, and rockets.

Date deployed:

First flight, November 1978;

Operational, October 1983 (A/B models); September 1987 (C/D models)

(Source: U.S. Navy Fact Files online)

EA-6B

EA-6B Prowler

The EA-6B Prowler is the U.S. Navy's electronic warfare aircraft adapted from the A-6 Intruder bomber. The Prowler jams radar, electronic data links, and communications to blind enemy air defenses during an attack. The Prowler, just like the Intruder, was designed for carrier operations, and carrier battle groups have been relying on this unique aircraft for electronic protection since Vietnam. It has a fully integrated electronic warfare system combining long-range, all-weather capabilities with advanced electronic counter-measures.

The pilot sits side by side with an ECM officer in a unique arrangement left over from the air-frame's A-6 days. The ECM officer replaces the Intruder's bombardier.

General Characteristics

Primary function: Electronic countermeasures
Contractor: Northrop Grumman Aerospace Corporation

Propulsion: Two Pratt & Whitney J52-P408 engines (10,400 pounds thrust each)
Length: 59 feet, 10 inches (17.7 meters)
Wingspan: 53 feet (15.9 meters)
Height: 16 feet, 8 inches (4.9 meters)
Weight: Max gross takeoff: 61,500 pounds (27,450 kilograms)
Speed: Over 500 knots (575 mph; 920 km/h)
Range: Over 1,000 nautical miles (1,150 miles; 1,840 kilometers)
Ceiling: 37,600 feet (11,460 meters)
Crew: Four: pilot and three electronic counter-measures officers
Armament: AGM-88B or HARM missile
Date deployed: First flight, May 25, 1968; Operational, July 1971
(Source: U.S. Navy Fact File)

Tornado Attack/Fighter Aircraft (U.K.)

The Tornado is a supersonic, variable geometry aircraft with two engines and two crew members, a pilot and a weapons systems officer. Designed

Tornado

for countering Warsaw Pact armored columns and for air strikes against enemy airfields, the Tornado must now face missions with improved enemy air defenses and engage more difficult targets. The Tornado is all-weather capable, and can use nuclear and conventional weapons systems, including the sophisticated laser-guided bombs, the antiarmor weapon Brimstone, and Britain's new cruise missile, the Storm Shadow.

General Characteristics

Country: Germany, Italy, United Kingdom

Manufacturer: Panavia Aircraft GmbH, Germany

Crew: Two: pilot and WSO (weapons systems operator)

Armament: Two internal 27mm Mauser cannon with 180 rounds per gun, plus more than 19,800 pounds (9,000 kilograms) of external stores on seven hardpoints, including Sidewinder, Texas Instruments HARM, Hughes AGM-65 Maverick, British Aerospace ALARM, laser-guided bombs like Paveway, bombs up to 1,000 pounds (450 kilograms), MW-1 munitions dispenser, Matra Apache, nuclear freefall bombs

Power plant: Two Turbo-Union RB199-34R turbofans

Thrust: 8,700 pounds dry and 14,480 pounds with afterburner

Length: 54.8 feet (16.72 meters)

Height: 19.5 feet (5.95 meters)

Wingspan: 45.6 feet (13.91 meters) fully forward, 28.2 feet (8.60 meters) fully swept

Wing area: 286 square feet (26.6 square meters)

Weights:

Empty weight: approximately 30,600 pounds (13,890 kilograms)

Maximum external load: over 19,820 pounds (9,000 kilograms)

Maximum fuel: 10,265 pounds (4,660 kilograms); 11,230 pounds (5,100 kilograms) in RAF and Saudi aircraft

Maximum takeoff weight: approximately 61,674 pounds (28,000 kilograms)

Performance: Maximum speed: 1,452 mph (2,336 km/h) at 36,000 feet (11,000 meters)

Maximum speed: Mach 2.2 at altitude; Mach 0.92 (688 mph; 1,110 km/h) with external stores

Rate of climb: Time to 30,000 feet (9,150 meters) less than two minutes

Takeoff field length: 2,950 feet (900 meters) or less

Landing run: 1,210 feet (370 meters)

Ferry range: approximately 2,418 miles (3,900 kilometers)

Radius of action: 862 miles (1,390 kilometers) with heavy load

g limit: 7.5-plus

Customers: The IDS (interdictor-strike) version of Tornado is in service with the British Royal Air Force, Luftwaffe, German navy, Italian air force, and Royal Saudi Air Force.

(Source: Federation of American Scientists, www. fas.org)

A-10 Thunderbolt

The A/OA-10 Thunderbolt II, affectionately called the Warthog due to its ungainly appearance, is specially designed for close air support of ground forces. Thunderbolts boast a prodigious suite of weaponry tailored to destroy tanks and other armored vehicles. This is yet another weapon system designed to attack Soviet and Warsaw Pact armor in the event of World War III in Europe. They are also effective against almost all ground targets.

They were particularly effective against the Iraqi SCUDs during the Persian Gulf War due to their long time over target and slow speed, making them ideal for ground support missions.

General Characteristics

Primary function: A-10, close air support; OA-10, airborne forward air control

Contractor: Fairchild Republic Co.

Power plant: Two General Electric TF34-GE-100 turbofans

Thrust: 9,065 pounds each engine

Length: 53 feet, 4 inches (16.16 meters)

Height: 14 feet, 8 inches (4.42 meters)

Wingspan: 57 feet, 6 inches (17.42 meters)

Speed: 420 mph (Mach 0.56; 677 km/h)

Ceiling: 45,000 feet (13,636 meters)

A-10

Department of Defense

Maximum takeoff weight: 51,000 pounds (22,950 kilograms)

Range: 800 miles (1,290 kilometers)

Armament: One 30mm GAU-8/A seven-barrel Gatling gun; up to 16,000 pounds (7,200 kilograms) of mixed ordnance on eight under-wing and three under-fuselage pylon stations, including 500 pounds (225 kilograms) of Mk-82 and 2,000 pounds (900 kilograms) of Mk-84 series low/high-drag bombs, incendiary cluster bombs, combined-effects munitions, mine dispensing munitions, AGM-65 Maverick missiles and laser-guided/electro-optically-guided bombs; infrared countermeasure flares; electronic countermeasure chaff; jammer pods; 2.75-inch (6.99-centimeter) rockets; illumination flares, and AIM-9 Sidewinder missiles.

Crew: One

Date deployed: March 1976

Unit cost: $9.8 million (fiscal 1998 constant dollars)

Inventory: Active force, A-10, 143, and OA-10, 70; ANG, A-10, 84, and OA-10, 18; Reserve, A-10, 46, and OA-10, 6

(Source: USAF Fact Sheets online)

AV-8B Harrier

The Harrier is the Marine Corps' primary close ground support aircraft. Like the A-10 it is designed to attack targets on the ground, but it can also engage enemy aircraft. With its unique fixed wing V/STOL (Vertical/Short Takeoff and Landing) design, it may be the most versatile fighting platform in the entire U.S. arsenal.

Louvers on the Harrier's engines can be shifted in order to change the direction of the engine's thrust from vertical to horizontal. This allows the plane to lift off like a helicopter, and then operate as a jet. Because of this unique feature, the Harrier can be based either on a ship or at an airbase.

During the Persian Gulf War the Harrier was the first Marine Corps tactical strike platform to

AV-8B Harrier

Department of Defense

arrive in station. It flew over 3,000 sorties over the course of the war and, in many cases, was deployed a mere 40 miles from the Kuwait border.

General Characteristics

Primary function: Multirole attack and close ground support aircraft

Contractor: McDonnell Douglas Aircraft (Airframe Prime), Rolls Royce (Engine Prime)

Power plant: One Rolls Royce Pegasus F402-RR-406 turbofan engine

Thrust: 20,280 pounds

Length: 46.3 feet (14.11 meters)

Wingspan: 30.3 feet (9.2 meters)

Cruise speed: Subsonic to transonic

Ferry range: 2,100 nautical miles (2,416.64 miles)

Combat radius:

Close air support: 163 nautical miles (187.45 miles) with 30 minutes time on station

Interdiction: 454 nautical miles (522.45 miles)

Armament: Seven external store stations, comprising six wing stations for AIM-9 Sidewinder and an assortment of air-to-ground weapons, external fuel tanks and AGM-65 Maverick missiles; one centerline station for DECM pod or air-to-ground ordnance. A GAU-12 25MM six-barrel gun pod can be mounted on the centerline and has a 300-round capacity with a lead computing optical sight system (LCOSS) gunsight

Crew: one

Introduction date: 12 January 1985; AV-8B11(Plus) introduced in June 1993

Unit replacement cost: $23.7 million

Missiles and Ordnance

AIM-120 Air-to-Air Missile (AMRAAM)

The AIM-120 advanced medium-range air-to-air missile (AMRAAM) is a new generation air-to-air missile designed to supplement the older Sidewinders and Sparrows. Inertial midcourse guidance and radar active homing give the AMRAAM an all-weather, beyond-visual-range capability. The AMRAAM is being procured for the U.S. Air Force, the U.S. Navy, and America's allies.

AIM-120

Robert F. Dorr

Primary function: Air-to-air tactical missile

Contractor: Hughes Aircraft Co. and Raytheon Co.

Power plant: High performance

Length: 143.9 inches (366 centimeters)

Launch weight: 335 pounds (150.75 kilograms)

Diameter: 7 inches (17.78 centimeters)

Wingspan: 20.7 inches (52.58 centimeters)

Range: 20-plus miles (32 kilometers)

Speed: Supersonic

Guidance system: Active radar terminal/inertial midcourse

Warhead: Blast fragmentation

Unit cost: $386,000

Date deployed: September 1991

(Source: USAF Fact Sheets online)

AGM-86C Conventional Air-Launched Cruise Missile— CALCM

The AGM-86C Conventional Air-Launched Cruise Missile (CALCM) was one of the developments that transformed the mission of the B-52H bombers. Rather than overfly a target, which can be extremely dangerous (B-52s were shot down over Vietnam), the CALCM allows this veteran bomber to stand off an enemy country's airspace and launch munitions at a distance.

Much like the buzz bombs of World War II, the jet-engined CALCM travels at subsonic speeds. After launch, the missile's folded wings, tail surfaces, and engine inlet deploy. The CALCM does not have to fly to a target in a straight line as a dumb bomb would do. It can fly an intricate route by using its Inertial Navigation System (INS) in concert with its onboard Global Positioning System (GPS). This allows the missile to guide itself with extreme accuracy to within a few feet of the target.

The CALCM allows greater target selection.

The B-52H can carry twelve CALCMs externally and eight internally on a rotary launcher, for a total of twenty CALCMs per aircraft. The CALCM carries only conventional munitions in place of the nuclear payload carried by its predecessor, the AGM-86B Air-Launched Cruise Missile (ALCM).

The CALCM is small and hard to detect on radar as it flies at low altitudes through the countryside. With air superiority on the Allies' side in a new war with Iraq, Saddam's defenders will not be able to attack these missiles from the air, which is the most effective way to defeat this weapon system. They will have to rely on surface-to-air missiles and antiaircraft guns. Without adequate early-warning radar, this type of defense will not be very effective.

General Characteristics

Primary function: Air-to-ground strategic cruise missile

Contractor: Boeing Defense & Space Group Aerojet—CALCM warhead

Guidance contractors: Litton Guidance & Control, Rockwell Collins Avionics, and Interstate Electronics Corp.

Power plant: Williams International Corp. F-107-WR-101 turbofan engine

Thrust: 600 pounds

Length: 20 feet, 9 inches (6.3 meters)

Weight: 3,250 pounds (1,475 kilograms)

Diameter: 24.5 inches (0.62 meters)

Wingspan: 12 feet (3.7 meters)

Range: Nominal: 600 nautical miles (840 kilometers); Specific: Classified

Speed: Nominal: High Subsonic; Specific: Classified

Guidance system: Litton Inertial Navigation Element integrated with an onboard Global Positioning System

Warhead: 1,500-pound (681-kilogram) AFX-760 blast fragmentation warhead; 3,000-pound (1,362-kilogram) PBXN-111 blast fragmentation warhead, penetrating warhead

Current inventory: approximately 100
Unit cost: $600,000 contract price
(Source: Federation of American Scientists, www. fas.org)

Tomahawk Cruise Missile

The Tomahawk is the U.S. Navy's long-range, land-attack cruise missile. It is launched from surface ships and can be launched from submarines. Tomahawks fly at very low altitudes at near Mach 1, and are guided over a predetermined route by a terrain-following/matching system with a GPS to aid in accuracy. Their first operational use was in Operation Desert Storm, in 1991, with great success. The missile has since been successfully used in several other conflicts and was used to attack Osama bin Laden's training facilities in Afghanistan as well as other targets during the Afghan War.

General Characteristics

Primary function: Long-range subsonic cruise missile for striking high-value or heavily defended land targets.

Contractor: Raytheon Systems Company
Power plant: Williams International F107-WR-402 cruise turbofan engine; CSD/ARC solid-fuel booster
Length: 18 feet, 3 inches (5.56 meters); with booster: 20 feet, 6 inches (6.25 meters)
Weight: 2,900 pounds (1,315 kilograms); 3,500 pounds (1,587 kilograms) with booster
Diameter: 20.4 inches (51.81 centimeters)
Wingspan: 8 feet, 9 inches (2.67 meters)
Range: 870 nautical miles (1,000 miles; 1,609 kilometers)
Speed: Subsonic, about 550 mph (880 km/h)
Guidance system: TERCOM, DSMAC, and GPS (Block III only)
Warheads: 1,000 pounds (454 kilograms) or conventional submunitions dispenser with combined-effect bomblets
Date deployed: 1986, IOC; 1994, Block III
Unit cost: approximately $600,000 (from the last production contract)
(Source: U.S. Navy Fact File online)

AGM-86C Cruise Missile

US Air Force

AGM-65 Air-to-Surface Missile—Maverick

The AGM-65 Maverick is what one might call a general-purpose air-to-surface guided missile for tactical use. The Maverick is used for enemy force suppression, close air support, and enemy force interdiction. It is a stand-off missile that can engage a host of tactical targets, including armor, air defenses, ships, transportation equipment, and fuel storage facilities.

General Characteristics

Primary function: Air-to-surface guided missile

Contractor: Raytheon Systems Co.

Power plant: Thiokol TX-481 solid-propellant rocket motor

Launch weight: AGM-65K, 793 pounds (360 kilograms)

Diameter: 1 foot (30.48 centimeters)

Wingspan: 2 feet, 4 inches (71.12 centimeters)

Range: Classified

Speed: Classified

Aircraft: Used aboard A-10, F-15E, and F-16

Guidance system: AGM-65B/K, electro-optical television; AGM-65D/F/G, imaging infrared; AGM-65E, laser guided

Warheads: AGM-65B/D, 125 pounds (56.25 kilograms), cone shaped; AGM-65E/F/G/K, 300 pounds (135 kilograms) delayed-fuse penetrator, heavyweight

Unit cost: $17,000 to $110,000 depending on the Maverick variant

Date deployed: August 1972

Inventory: Classified

(Source: USAF Fact Sheets online)

US Air Force

AGM-114 Air-to-Surface Missile—Hellfire

Hellfire is a laser-guided missile designed for anti-tank missions. It also has air-to-air capability against slow-moving, fixed-wing, or rotor aircraft.

The Hellfire missile can destroy any tank in the world. It follows laser light from its own aircraft, another aircraft, or ground laser designation sources. This missile can also be used against hardened structures, such as bunkers, command posts, and fortified buildings. The Hellfire was used extensively during the Persian Gulf War and was fired from helicopters against Iraqi armor.

General Characteristics

Primary function: Point target/antiarmor weapon, semiactive laser seeker
Three variants: AGM-114B/K/M
Contractors: Boeing, Lockheed Martin
Power plant: solid-propellant rocket
Length: 5.33 feet (1.6 meters)
Launch weight: 98 to 107 pounds (44 to 48.5 kilograms)
Diameter: 7 inches (17.8 centimeters)
Wingspan: 28 inches (0.71 meter)
Speed: Subsonic
Warhead: Shaped charge and blast fragmentation
Aircraft platforms:
Navy: SH-60B/HH-60H Seahawk;
Army: AH-64 Apache;
Marine: AH-1W Super Cobra
(Source: U.S. Navy Fact File online)

BGM-71 Tube-Launched Optically-Tracked Wire-Guided Missile—TOW

The TOW is a wire-guided, antiarmor missile developed for use in a possible confrontation with Soviet and Warsaw Pact armor in Europe. The weapon system can be man-portable or vehicle-mounted on Humvees and Bradley Fighting Vehicles. TOW is capable of engaging armor and hardened targets, such as field fortifications, from distances greater than two miles. After launch, the gunner must keep the sight on the target and guide the missile to the target. The system will operate in all weather conditions as long as the gunner can see the target during the entire missile flight via day or night sight.

General Characteristics

Primary function: Guided missile weapon system
Manufacturer: Hughes (missiles); Hughes and Kollsman (night sights); Electro Design Mfg. (launchers)
Size (TOW 2B missile):
Diameter: 5.8 inches (14.9 centimeters)
Length: 48.0 inches (121.9 centimeters)
Warhead weight: 27.3 pounds (12.4 kilograms)
Maximum effective range: 2.33 miles (3.75 kilometers)
Time of flight to maximum effective range: 2A: 20 seconds; 2B: 21 seconds
Weight:
Launcher w/TOW 2 mods: 204.6 pounds (92.9 kilograms)
Missile guidance set: 52.8 pounds (24 kilograms)
TOW 2B missile: 49.8 pounds (22.6 kilograms)
Introduction date: 1970
Unit replacement cost: $180,000
Launching platforms: Man-portable crew of four, HMMWV, M2/M3 Bradley Fighting Vehicle
Marine Corps inventory: TOW launchers, 1,247
(Source: Federation of American Scientists, www.fas.org)

AGM-88 High-Speed Antiradiation Missile—HARM

The AGM-88 HARM is a tactical, supersonic, air-to-surface missile designed to destroy enemy radar

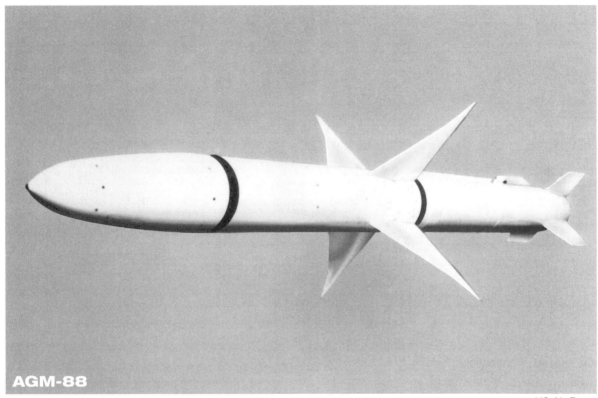

AGM-88

US Air Force

by following the radar's electromagnetic signals back toward the radar's antenna.

Minimum aircrew intervention is needed for the HARM to detect, attack, and destroy a target. The HARM has a smokeless, solid-propellant, dual-thrust rocket motor. The F-16C is the only aircraft in the current inventory to use the AGM-88.

General Characteristics

Primary function: Air-to-surface antiradiation missile
Contractor: Texas Instruments
Power plant: Thiokol dual-thrust rocket motor
Thrust: Dual thrust
Length: 13 feet, 8 inches (4.14 meters)
Launch weight: 800 pounds (360 kilograms)
Diameter: 10 inches (25.40 centimeters)
Wingspan: 3 feet, 8 inches (101.60 centimeters)
Range: 30-plus miles (48-plus kilometers)
Speed: Supersonic

Aircraft: Used aboard the F-16C
Guidance system: Proportional
Warheads: High explosive
Unit cost: $200,000
Date deployed: 1984
(Source: USAF Fact Sheets online)

AGM-45 Antiradiation Missile—Shrike

The Shrike is an older antiradiation missile designed to home in on hostile antiaircraft radars. It is currently used by U.S. and Israeli air forces.

General Characteristics

Primary function: Antiradiation missile that homes in on hostile antiaircraft radars
Propulsion: Solid-fuel rocket
Length: 10 feet (3.1 meters)
Weight: 390 pounds (177 kilograms)
Diameter: 8 inches (20.3 centimeters)

43

AGM-45

US Navy

Warhead: Conventional
Span: 3 feet (0.9 meters)
Guidance: Passive radar homing
Platforms: A-4 Skyhawk, A-6 Intruder
Unit replacement cost: $32,000
(Source: U.S. Marine Corps Fact File online)

AGM-158 Joint Air-to-Surface Standoff Missile—JASSM

JASSM is a guided cruise missile, launched from beyond enemy territory to attack hardened and other targets. The aircraft platforms include most of the U.S. Air Force and Navy inventory, including the P-3 Orion and the Viking antisub aircraft. The JASSM flies to the target using an inertial guidance system aided by a GPS receiver system with a high-gain, antijam, null steering antenna. It autonomously flies a low-level, circuitous route to the target, where an imaging infrared camera matches a target's pattern with a stored image of the target. When a match is detected, the missile attacks the target.

General Characteristics

Targets: Hard, medium-hardened, soft, and area-fixed and relocatable targets
Service: Air Force
Guidance method: Global Positioning System (GPS)–aided Inertial Navigation System (INS)
Production unit cost: $700,000
Platforms: B-52 (12) FY01, B-1 (24) FY02, B-2 (16) FY03, F-16 (2) FY04, F-16C/D, F/A-18E/F F-15E, F-117, P-3C, S-3B
(Source: Federation of American Scientists, www. fas.org)

Patriot (PAC-3) Surface-to-Air Missile System

Originally designed as a surface-to-air missile system against aircraft, the Patriot was reprogrammed to attack missiles during their reentry phase as a terminal missile defense weapon. The Patriot was used during the Persian Gulf War to defend against Iraq's SCUD missiles as the warheads reentered the earth's atmosphere. Patriots provided stirring images as they raced to attack SCUDs before the warheads impacted on random

Patriot Missile

US Army

targets. Performance of the Patriots against the SCUDs was initially deemed wildly successful. Then when videotape was examined after the war, it was concluded that no evidence existed that the Patriot missile intercepted any warheads. Most of what was hit by the Patriot was the SCUD missile bodies that reentered along with the warhead. The missile bodies broke up as they reentered and created a larger target for the Patriot's radar. The smaller warhead among all the debris was hardly, if ever, hit by the Patriot missile. The Patriots were designed to explode close to a target and use shrapnel to destroy it.

Since the Persian Gulf War, the United States has come out with the Patriot Advanced Capability-3 (PAC-3) as the latest version to counter the SCUD missile threat. Since August 2002, about thirty-six PAC-3 missiles have been deliv-

ered—or enough to deploy two army air defense batteries. Patriot has major software upgrades that provide four times greater computer power throughput.

The new PAC-3 missile is designed as a hit-to-kill weapon system against ballistic missiles, cruise missiles, maneuvering tactical missiles, and combat aircraft. PAC-3 uses an active radar seeker in a closed-loop system to directly hit the target. The active radar seeker in the Patriot has a complete radar system in the missile itself, rather than relying upon the ground radar to illuminate the target. PAC-3 also includes a new interceptor missile for enhanced performance.

During the Persian Gulf War, Saddam's military obligingly sent SCUDs over one at a time without decoys (except for the broken-up missile bodies) and without any attempted jamming of the Patriot's radar. One tactic Iraq might use is to try to overwhelm missile defenses by using many missiles simultaneously. Decoys and in-flight jamming are probably beyond Iraq's current capabilities.

Bunker Busters—GBU-28

When the command and control bunkers at Al-Taji airbase were targeted during the Persian Gulf War, the U.S. Air Force dropped 2,000-pound bombs on them to no effect. The U.S. military knew it needed a special penetrating bomb, not yet in the U.S. inventory, to destroy these targets. In a very short period of time, a design was crafted using available materials to create two bombs for use at Al-Taji.

Eight-inch artillery barrels were used as the bomb casings and 630 pounds of Tritonal were poured in. The bombs were fitted with the laser-guided system used on the GBU-27. A laser designator operator shines laser light on the target, the reflected light is received by the bomb's receiver, and the laser guide unit operates the bomb fins to guide the bomb to the target.

Two of these weapons were dropped on the deep underground bunkers at Al-Taji by F-111s. One missed, and one hit perfectly, penetrating the roof, with the explosion's effects seen some seven seconds later.

General Characteristics

Mission: Offensive counter air, close air support, interdiction
Targets: Fixed hard
Class: 4,000-pound Penetrator, blast fragmentation
Service: Air Force
Contractor: Lockheed Martin (BLU-113/B), National Forge (BLU-113A/B)
First capability: 1991
Weight: 4,414 pounds (2,000 kilograms)
Length: 153 inches (3.9 meters)
Diameter: 14.5 inches (0.4 meters)

Explosive: 647 pounds (294 kilograms) Tritonal
Fuse: FMU-143 Series
Stabilizer: Air Foil Group (Fins)
Guidance method: Laser (man-in-the-loop)
Range: Greater than 5 nautical miles (9.3 kilometers)
Production unit cost: $145,600
Quantity: 125 plus additional production
Platforms: F-15E, F-111F
(Source: Federation of American Scientists, www. fas.org)

Bunker Busters— 30,000-Pound Bomb

This bomb is the largest conventional munition in the U.S. arsenal. It is designed to defeat the tactic of placing hardened bunkers ever deeper underground for command and control facilities, intelligence centers, and strategic headquarters. It is designed to be dropped by a B-2 stealth bomber.

BLU-118 Thermobaric Warhead

The Bomb Live Unit (BLU)-118/B is designed for deep underground bunkers and features a penetrating warhead of a thermobaric explosive, which stretches out the blast pressure pulse by releasing intense energy over a longer time period. This will create greater destructive forces in confined spaces such as tunnels and underground facilities. These warheads are compatible with the current Guided Bomb Unit (GBU)-15, GBU-24, and air-launched surface-attack guided missile (AGM)-130 weapon systems that are used on the F-15E Strike Eagle aircraft.

CBU-97/CBU-105 Sensor-Fused Weapon

The CBU-97 is an antiarmor cluster weapon that contains submunitions with infrared sensors that deploy over an area of about 500 feet by 1,200 feet. Each weapon contains ten submunitions on parachutes with four hockey-puck-shaped, armor-penetrating projectiles each. When a target is detected, explosives fire the projectiles at the target. If no target is detected, the submunitions will detonate after a preprogrammed amount of time. This munition would be used against armor columns for disruption purposes in the early stages of a confrontation with a belligerent country.

General Characteristics

Weight: 927 pounds (421 kilograms)
Length: 92 inches (2.3 meters)
Diameter: 16 inches (0.4 meters)
Guidance: None
Control: None
Autopilot: None
Propulsion: None
Warhead: SUU-66/B tactical munitions dispenser; 10 BLU-108/B submunitions, each with 4 projectiles
Fuse: Integral part of dispenser; FZU-39/B proximity sensor
Aircraft: 12 F-15E, 4 F-16, 10 A-10, 30 B-1, 34 B-2, 16 B-52
Limitations: 200 feet to 20,000 feet (above ground level; 61 to 6,100 meters)
Delivery envelope: 250 knots to 650 knots (464 to 1,205 km/h)
Unit cost: $360,000, baseline; $260,000, PEP $39,963 (fiscal 1990 constant dollars)
Inventory: 500 in USAF inventory as of 01/01/1998; current USAF objective is 5,000 (17,000 originally planned)
(Source: Federation of American Scientists, www. fas.org)

CBU-72—Fuel-Air Explosives (FAE)

Originally used in Vietnam, this weapon is used against minefields, armor, aircraft, and entrenched enemy personnel. This 550-pound weapon is a cluster bomb containing three fuel-air explosive (FAE) submunitions. The submunitions detonate at approximately thirty feet above ground. The fuel is seventy-five pounds of ethylene oxide. An aerosol cloud approximately sixty feet in diameter and eight feet thick is created, then ignited to produce an explosion.

During the Persian Gulf War this weapon was used by the U.S. Marine Corps, dropped from Intruders against minefields and enemy troops in trenches.

General Characteristics

Weight: 500 pounds (227 kilograms)
Length: 85.6 inches (2.2 meters)
Diameter: 14 inches (0.36 meter)
Guidance: None
Control: None
Autopilot: None
Propulsion: None
Warhead: 3 BLU-73/B fuel
Fuse: Mark 339 Mod 0 Mechanical
(Source: Federation of American Scientists, www.fas.org)

CBU-94 Blackout Bomb and BLU-114/B Soft Bomb

The Blackout bomb was first used against the Serbs during the Bosnia War to short out power plants and deprive large areas of electricity without greatly destroying electrical infrastructure or taking civilian lives. Not much is known about this highly classified weapon, but it seems to eject submunitions, which detonate, spraying a cloud of thin carbon wires over an area. The carbon wires settle over a power plant's exposed wires and contacts, causing large currents to flow through the wires, resulting in arcing. This will melt electrical components, including contactors, cables, and transformers. The F-117A Nighthawk was used in Serbia to drop these munitions.
(Source: Federation of American Scientists, www.fas.org)

Land Forces

M1A1 Abrams Main Battle Tank

The M1A1 is a very large, heavily armored main battle tank with state-of-the-art firepower, target acquisition, infrared sights, and laser aiming system. The M1A1 can engage enemy targets almost to 2.5 miles (4,000 meters), as was shown during the Persian Gulf War. It can fire its 120mm smoothbore main gun with high accuracy while moving because of a high-tech gun stabilization system, which keeps the gun aimed at the target despite what the tank body is doing.

One disadvantage of the M1A1 is its prodigious gas usage by its gas turbine engine. These tanks have to continually circle back to refuel, and moving enormous quantities of gasoline through Iraq, fording streams and rivers, and surmounting wadis is a daunting task. As coalition armor moves into hostile territory, its supply lines grow ever longer, inviting attack from small, quick-moving enemy forces. This, coupled with the fact that the gasoline trucks are not armored, could produce the U.S. armor's Achilles' heel. If the Iraqis could attack enough of the M1s' supply lines, it could slow down or even bring the advance of U.S. armor to a halt.

General Characteristics

Primary function: Main battle tank (MBT)
Manufacturer: General Dynamics (Land Systems Division)
Power plant: AGT-1500 turbine engine

M1A1 Abrams

US Army

Power train: Hydrokinetic, fully automatic with four forward and two reverse gear ratios

Propulsion: 1,500-horsepower gas (multifuel) turbine engine

Length, gun forward: 385 inches (9.78 meters)

Width: 144 inches (3.66 meters)

Height: 114 inches (2.89 meters) without DWFK (Deep Water Fording Kit)

Weight fully armed: 67.7 tons (61.4 metric tons)

Caliber: 120mm (M256 main gun)

Commander's weapon: M2 .50-caliber machine gun

Loader's weapon: 7.62mm M240 machine gun

Coaxial weapon: 7.62mm M240 machine gun

Cruising range: 289 miles (465 kilometers) without NBC (nuclear, biological, and chemical) protection system; 279 miles (449 kilometers) with NBC system

Sight radius: 8 degrees at 8× power

Speed:
Maximum: 42 mph (67.7 km/h) governed
Cross country: 30 mph (48.3 km/h)

Ground clearance: 19 inches (48.26 centimeters)

Obstacle crossing:
Vertical: 42 inches (106.68 centimeters)
Trench: 9 feet wide (2.7 meters)
Slope: 60 degrees at 4.5 miles (7.2 kilometers) per hour

Crew: A four-man crew composed of a driver, loader, gunner, and tank commander

Warheads: M1A1 tank is capable of delivering both kinetic energy (sabot) and chemical energy (heat) rounds.

Armament:
Main: 120mm M256 main gun
Secondary: (1) .50-caliber M2 machine guns; (2) 7.62mm M240 machine guns

Sensors: The 120mm M256 main gun has a cant sensor, wind-speed sensor, automatic lead and ammunition temperature inputs to its ballistic fire control solution.

Introduction date: November 1990

Unit replacement cost: $4.3 million

(Source: USMC information online)

Challenger 2 Main Battle Tank (U.K.)

The Challenger is the main battle tank for the United Kingdom. The main gun is a 120mm rifled tank gun. The Challenger also has a McDonnell Douglas Helicopter Systems 7.62mm chain gun, and a 7.62mm antiaircraft machine gun. The Challenger has improved armor plating and fire control system compared to that in the U.S. M1A1 Abrams tank.

The Challenger 2 carries a crew of four, a commander, driver, gunner, and loader. It has a maximum road speed of 35 miles per hour (56 km/h), a bit slower than the M1A1, and a range of 155 miles (250 kilometers) cross country and 279 miles (450 kilometers) on the road, comparable to the M1A1.

Its nuclear, biological, and chemical (NBC) protection system can deal with all known agents.

General Characteristics

Combat weight: 68.8 tons (62,500 kilograms)

Crew size: Four

Length (hull): 27 feet (8.3 meters)

Length (gun forward): 38 feet (11.6 meters)

Width (over skirts): 11.5 feet (3.5 meters)

Height (to turret roof): 8.2 feet (2.5 meters)

Ground clearance: 1.6 feet (0.5 meters)

Maximum road range: 279 miles (450 kilometers)

Engine: Rolls-Royce Perkins Condor CV12 1,200bhp with new engine management system

Gearbox: David Brown TN54 epicyclic, 6 forward, 2 reverse

Suspension: Hydrogas variable spring rate

Track: Blair Catton hydraulically adjusted double pin

Speed: 35 mph road (56 km/h); 25 mph mean cross country (40 km/h)

Main armament: Royal Ordnance 120mm L30 gun

Ammunition: CHARM 1 and 3, HESH and Smoke

Ammunition carried: Typically 50 rounds, APFSDS, HESH, Smoke

Secondary armament: Hughes 7.62mm coaxially mounted chain gun and 7.62mm loader's GPMG turret mounted for air defense

Ammunition carried: 4,000 rounds 7.62mm

Armor: Dorchester

Smoke dischargers: Exhaust smoke injection and two sets of five L8 grenade dischargers

Commander: Gyrostabilized fully panoramic sight with laser range finder and thermal imager

Gunner: Gyrostabilized primary sight with laser range finder and thermal imager, and coaxially mounted auxiliary sight

Driver: Day and night periscopes

Loader: Day periscope

M2 Bradley Fighting Vehicle

Named after General Omar Bradley, known as the GI General, the M2 Bradley Fighting Vehicle (BFV) is a tracked, armored vehicle designed to carry five or six troops into close proximity with the enemy. It performs as a highly sophisticated weapons platform capable of providing tremendous firepower to support the infantry it carries. The Bradley is capable of engaging enemy tanks, including the best tank the Iraqis have, the T-72, with its TOW

Bradley Fighting Vehicle

Robert F. Dorr

antiarmor missiles. This vehicle proved itself in combat in the Persian Gulf War.

General Characteristics

	M2 IFV	M3 CFV
Crew:	Three, plus Six infantry dismounts	Three, plus Two cavalry scouts

Length: 21 feet, 2 inches (6.5 meters)
Width: 10 feet, 6 inches (3.2 meters)
Height: 9 feet, 9 inches (3 meters)
Weight: 50,000 pounds (22,700 kilograms)
Road speed: 45 mph (73 km/h)
Range: 300 miles (484 kilometers)
Engine: Cummins VTA-903T water-cooled 4-cycle diesel
Armament: 25mm cannon (chain gun); 7.62mm coaxially mounted machine gun; TOW missile launcher with twin tubes
Inventory: 1,602 systems
Average unit cost: $3.166 million

Prime contractor: United Defense, Limited Partnership
(Source: Federation of American Scientists, www. fas.org)

M109A6 Paladin— Self-Propelled Artillery

The Paladin is a tracked, mobile 155mm self-propelled artillery weapon. The system features onboard navigational and automatic fire control systems. Paladin has a Kevlar-lined chassis to protect against shrapnel and small-arms fire and an NBC (nuclear, biological, chemical) protection system, featuring a pressurized crew compartment.

The M109A6 is the most technologically advanced cannon in the U.S. Army inventory. The Paladin's automatic systems give it the capability of firing on the move, then moving quickly from the area to avoid counterbattery fire from Iraqi gunners. It operates independently of any other system by receiving fire missions, computing firing data and

Paladin Howitzer

Robert F. Dorr

trajectories, taking up its firing position, and pointing and firing its cannon using its own internal fire control systems. The Paladin features day/night capability with secure voice and digital communications.

General Characteristics

Weapon size: 155mm
Weapon range: 18.6 miles (30 kilometers)
Firing rate: 4 rounds per minute
Weight: 62,000 pounds/32 tons (28,150 kilograms)
Speed: 35 mph (56.5 km/h) maximum
Cruising range: 186 miles (300 kilometers)
Crew: Four
(Source: Federation of American Scientists, www. fas.org)

AH-64A Apache Helicopter

The Apache is designed to engage armor and is yet another of the U.S. military's tank-killing weapons systems. The Apache can pop up from behind a hill, fire its Hellfire missiles, and drop back down before enemy gunners can lock on to it. It has day or night and adverse-weather capability, and the pilot uses an integrated helmet and display sight system. The AH-64A has advanced target acquisition designation sights, pilot night-vision system, radar jammer, infrared countermeasures, and nap-of-earth navigation, along with GPS navigation.

A disadvantage of this system is the enormous amount of ground support needed to make this aircraft effective in combat.

Apache

US Army

Length: 58.3 feet (17.8 meters) with rotors
Wingspan: 16.3 feet (5 meters)
Width: 6.5 feet (2 meters)
Height: 12.7 feet (3.9 meters)
Weight: 10.5 tons (9,534 kilograms)
Speed: 227 mph (366 km/h)
Range: 300 miles (484 kilometers)
Crew: Two
Armament: (various combinations) Hellfire missiles, Hydra 70 rocket, 30mm chain gun
(Source: U.S. Army online)

Infantry Weapons and Protective Gear

SMAW—Shoulder-Launched Multipurpose Assault Weapon

The SMAW is a man-portable, shoulder-fired weapon designed to engage light armored vehicles, bunkers, and other enemy fortifications with the high-explosive, dual-purpose (HEDP) rocket. The SMAW can also engage and destroy enemy main battle tanks with the HEAA rocket.

The launcher is a fiberglass tube loaded from the rear, which is reminiscent of the old bazooka of World War II days. The weapon is aimed through optical or night sights. The SMAW has a 9mm spotting rifle, an electromechanical firing mechanism, and open battle sights. The spotting rifle is a British design and is mounted on the right side of the launch tube. The operator first fires the spotting round, and when he hits the desired spot on the target, he fires the rocket. The rocket will hit the target at the same point as the spotting round, because the rockets are ballistically matched to the spotting rounds. This dramatically increases the probability of hitting the target on the first shot.

Primary function: Portable antiarmor rocket launcher
Length: To carry: 29.9 inches (76 centimeters); Ready to fire: 54 inches (137.2 centimeters)
Weight: To carry: 16.6 pounds (7.5 kilograms); Ready to fire (HEDP): 29.5 pounds (13.4 kilograms); Ready to fire (HEAA): 30.5 pounds (13.9 kilograms)
Bore diameter: 83mm
Maximum effective range: 1-x-2-meter target: 820 feet (250 meters); tank-sized target: 1,640 feet (500 meters)
Introduction date: 1984
Unit replacement cost: $13,000
(Source: Federation of American Scientists, www. fas.org)

Biological and Chemical Warfare Protection

After the Persian Gulf War, the U.S. Army, Navy, Air Force, and Marines began a program to replace the then-current Chemical Protection Overgarment (CPO), a Mission-Oriented Protective Posture (MOPP) suit. The problems with the CPO were difficulty of movement, the suit could not be laundered, and the internal charcoal lining would come off onto a wearer's underclothes. Plus the effectiveness of the suit over sustained periods was in question.

The Joint Service Lightweight Integrated Suit Technology (JSLIST) garment is designed to solve the problems with the previous protective gear. It will replace the CPO, and will feature state-of-the-art chemical protective lining technology, which increases chemical protection, allows increased personnel mobility, and can be laundered up to three times.
(Source: Federation of American Scientists, www. fas.org)

Naval Power

Aircraft Carriers

The USS *Abraham Lincoln* is a Nimitz-class carrier capable of enormous firepower. Its air wing of more than eighty aircraft can project power around the globe, traveling to and from trouble spots and supporting U.S. military operations worldwide. In another Iraqi war, the navy's carrier aircraft will be used to attack targets around Iraq.

Carriers travel in carrier battle groups consisting of two cruisers, one or both with the Aegis system of integrated target engagement, along with several destroyers, frigates and support ships, and at least one attack submarine. The main threat to a carrier is no longer from the air but from the sea. Modern homing torpedoes, sub-launched cruise missiles, and antiship missiles create problems in defending the enormous aircraft carrier. Carriers are not stealthy and provide an enemy a very strong radar cross section. The navy's strategy for carrier group protection is defense in depth, from combat air patrols (CAP) to picket defense from its destroyers, and undersea protection from antisub helicopters on its frigates and its escorting submarines.

Iraqi chances of attacking carrier battle groups are near zero due to the decimation of the Iraqi navy during the Persian Gulf War.

General Characteristics

Purpose: Project airpower at trouble spots around the globe
Length: 1,108 feet (338 meters)
Height: 206 feet, 6 inches (63 meters)
Breadth: 257 feet, 5 inches (78.5 meters)
Flight deck: 4.5 acres
Displacement: 97,500 tons
Power: Nuclear, 2 reactors
Main engines: Four

Nimitz-class Aircraft Carrier

US Navy

Propellers: 4, 11 tons each
Rudders: 2, 45.5 tons each
Maximum speed: 30-plus knots
Air wing: 80-plus aircraft
Complement: 4,800-plus personnel
(Source: The Federation of American Scientists, www.fas.org, and U.S. Navy online)

Persian Gulf Theater Forces

Conventional

A current estimate of the forces arrayed against Saddam Hussein is listed below. The list shows a very formidable force, and it is increasing in size and capability all the time. Land forces will increase to approximately 250,000 troops and over 1,000 tanks. The U.S. Air Force will increase its aircraft to about 800. The U.S. Navy will provide 4 carrier battle groups, including approximately 320 carrier-based aircraft. The U.S. Marine Corps is providing marine expeditionary groups on land and afloat.

These forces surround Iraq from the Mediterranean Sea to the Persian Gulf and from Turkey in the north to Saudi Arabia and the Red Sea in the south.

Kuwait

U.S. Forces
3rd Brigade, 3rd Infantry Division (Mechanized)
  5,000 troops
  116 M1A1 main battle tanks
  60 M2A2 Bradley Fighting Vehicles
  25 M109A6 Paladin artillery pieces
  100 armored personnel carriers

3 aviation battalions
  75 helicopters

3 squadrons of the 6th Cavalry Regiment task force
  Apache attack helicopters
  UH-60 transport helicopters

A Special Forces company (100–200 personnel)
A Military Intelligence Brigade
USMC 11th Marine Expeditionary Unit
USAF 332nd Aerospace Expeditionary Group (AEG)
USAF 386th Aerospace Expeditionary Group
3,000 Air Force personnel supporting Operation Southern Watch
Total number of U.S. military personnel in Kuwait is over 10,000.

U.K. Forces
The British 1st Armoured Division (20,000 personnel)
12 Squadron, British Royal Air Force (RAF) Tornado GR.4

Jordan

1,400 U.S. Special Operations troops

Saudi Arabia

USAF 363rd Air Expeditionary Group
British Royal Air Force Tornado F.3 fighters

Persian Gulf

Task Force 50
  destroyers
  frigates
  1 submarine
USS *Abraham Lincoln* (CVN 72), nuclear aircraft carrier
USS *Shiloh* (CG 67), cruiser
USS *Mobile Bay* (CG 53), cruiser
USS *Fletcher* (DD 992), destroyer
USS *Paul Hamilton* (DDG 60), destroyer
USS *Reuben James* (FFG 57), frigate
USS *Honolulu* (SSN 718), attack submarine
USS *Camden* (AOE 2), combat support ship
USS *Belleau Wood* (LHA3), amphibious assault ship
USS *Mount Vernon* (LSD 39), amphibious assault ship

USS *Denver* (LPD 9), amphibious transport
    dock ship
USS *Ardent* (MCM 12), minesweeper
USS *Cardinal* (MHC 60), minesweeper
USS *Dextrous* (MCM 13), minesweeper
USS *Raven* (MHC 61), minesweeper

Red Sea

USS *Nassau* (LHA 4), amphibious assault
    ship
USMC 24th Marine Expeditionary Group
USS *Tortuga* (LSD 46), amphibious assault
    ship
USS *Austin* (LPD 4), amphibious transport
    dock ship

Mediterranean Sea

USS *George Washington* (CVN 73), nuclear
aircraft carrier and battle group
    2 cruisers
    2 destroyers
    1 or more frigates
    1 or more attack submarines
    1 support ship
USS *Constellation* (CV 64), aircraft carrier and
battle group
    2 cruisers
    2 destroyers
    1 or more frigates
    1 or more attack submarines
    1 support ship

Bahrain

U.S. Navy P-3 Orion antisubmarine and
    surveillance aircraft
SEAL Naval Special Warfare Unit 3
U.K. refueling tankers

Qatar

USAF 379th Air Expeditionary Wing
Unknown number of fighter/bomber aircraft

11 air-to-air refueling aircraft
JSTARS reconnaissance aircraft

United Arab Emirates (UAE)

USAF 380th Air Expeditionary Wing
Three reconnaissance squadrons
    Global Hawk reconnaissance unmanned
    aerial vehicles
Air Refueling Squadron, providing KC-135s
    for air-to-air refueling support

Oman

U.S. Forces
    355th Air Expeditionary Group
    1 squadron of AC-130 gunships
    405th Air Expeditionary Wing
    B-1 bombers
U.K. and Australian Forces
    1 squadron, British Special Forces elite
    Special Air Service
    2 P-3 Orion maritime reconnaissance aircraft
    of the Royal Australian Air Force

Turkey

Incirlik Air Base
    39th Wing (4,000 personnel)
    50 F-15 fighters
    A-10 ground attack aircraft
    F-16 fighters
    U.S. Navy EA-6 Prowler electronic warfare
    aircraft

Diego Garcia

40th Air Expeditionary Wing
    B-52 bombers
    B-2 stealth bombers
U.S. Navy P-3 Orion maritime patrol and
    surveillance force

Djibouti

800 U.S. troops, including Special Operations forces

Intelligence

Northern Iraq

2 CIA field offices in Kurdish territory

Special Forces

Western Iraq

Israeli Special Forces Unit 262 hunting SCUD missile launchers

Hungary

Up to 12,000 Iraqis are being brought to Hungary to be trained to go along with U.S. and Allied troops as interpreters and guides in an invasion of Iraq.

(Sources: The Center for Defense Information online, and ABC News, *November 26, 2002)*

Special Forces— Owning the Night

U.S. and U.K. Special Forces were very active during the Gulf War. They were inserted into Iraqi territory to gather intelligence about Iraqi ground forces, their positions, number, composition, battle readiness, number and types of vehicles, armor, and artillery pieces. They were dropped into enemy territory using stealth parachutes, gliding for many miles, hovering near enemy units, observing from above, and reporting back through special radios. They were inserted using MD-500s, special helicopters with silenced rotors that fly only feet above the desert. Others were flown in using MC-130 Combat Talon aircraft, all at night and in total darkness.

The Special Forces own the night. Looking through night-vision goggles, they maneuver at night—they fight at night. But much of what they do is to observe, intercept communications using handheld radios, and sometimes kidnap enemy soldiers to interrogate when they return to base. They are the eyes and ears of field commanders when faced with an enemy force. They find wadis or any crease in the desert floor to settle into, or dig holes to hide in, and using small periscopes they gather the information dearly needed by their comrades in arms. They live in these holes for days at a time. The enemy can pass right over them, stepping right on them, and not know they were there. Special Forces units report back using portable satellite communications gear, which transmits in very short bursts to avoid enemy direction finding on their radio transmission.

Britain's Special Air Service went into the western Iraqi desert to locate SCUD launchers and to place taps on Iraqi fiber-optic cables that crisscrossed the area. The launchers, and command and communications sites as well, were illuminated by target designators, which flashed a coded laser light on the target. Warplanes above would detect the laser light, read the code, and drop a laser-guided bomb on the target. Other SAS units traversed the desert dressed as Bedouins to avoid detection, all the while gathering intelligence.

U.S. Army Green Berets entered Kuwait City and Baghdad posing as salesmen from other countries, selling food and spare parts. Other Special Forces, some from the U.S. Marines, used target designators to aid attack aircraft in finding tanks, combat vehicles, communications towers, and other targets in the desert. Other units blew up bridges to attempt to prevent the vaunted Iraqi Republican Guard from escaping the theater of war.

The Special Forces world is a tightly disciplined one, of covert movements mostly at night and of concealment by day. They carry everything with them, even their own excrement, to avoid being tracked by the enemy.

Air Force Special Operations Command—AFSOC

This command is a component of the U.S. Special Operations Command under which all Special Operations are conducted with the exception of the Delta Force. The AFSOC provides air support to U.S. and Allied Special Forces. Special Forces are ferried into and out of enemy territory using a host of special aircraft, from small helicopters to large transport aircraft, the MH-53 Pave Low, MH-47E Chinook, MH-60 Black Hawk helicopters, along with the MD-500 series of small helicopters. Special Forces are supported by the AC-130 Spectre gunship, which is an artillery platform in the sky. The Spectre is armed with two 20mm Gatling guns, a 40mm cannon, and a 105mm howitzer. This provides considerable mobile fire support. For transport at low levels, the MC-130 Combat Talon aircraft is used primarily at night. Pilots wear night-vision goggles and takeoffs and landings are executed in the complete dark. The Combat Talon is optimized for short takeoffs and landings.

MC-130 Combat Talon

The MC-130E Combat Talon I and MC-130H Combat Talon II aircraft are used to insert and extract Special Forces behind enemy lines. The aircraft are optimized for low-level flying. The Combat Talon crews are trained to take off and land in total darkness with perhaps only an infrared marker operated by Special Forces to guide the air crew. The aircraft can also be used in helicopter refueling and in psychological operations.

General Characteristics

Primary function: Infiltration, exfiltration, and resupply of Special Operations forces
Builder: Lockheed Martin
Power plant: Four Allison T56-A-15 turboprop engines
Thrust: 4,910 shaft horsepower each engine
Length:
MC-130E: 100 feet, 10 inches (30.7 meters)
MC-130H: 99 feet, 9 inches (30.4 meters)
Height: 38 feet, 6 inches (11.7 meters)

MC-130 Combat Talon

US Air Force

Wingspan: 132 feet, 7 inches (40.4 meters)

Speed: 300 mph (484 km/h)

Load:

MC-130E: 53 troops, 26 paratroopers

MC-130H: 77 troops, 52 paratroopers or 57 litter patients

Ceiling: 33,000 feet (10,000 meters)

Maximum takeoff weight: 155,000 pounds (69,750 kilograms)

Range: 2,700 nautical miles (5,000 kilometers); in-flight refueling extends this to unlimited range

Crew:

MC-130E: Officers—two pilots, two navigators, and an electronic warfare officer; enlisted—flight engineer, radio operator, and two loadmasters

MC-130H: Officers—two pilots, a navigator, and electronic warfare officer; enlisted—flight engineer and two loadmasters

Date deployed: MC-130E, 1966; MC-130H, June 1991

Unit cost: MC-130E, $75 million; MC-130H, $155 million (fiscal 2001 constant dollars)

Inventory: Active force, MC-130H, 24; ANG, 0; Reserve, MC-130E, 14

(Source: USAF Fact Sheets online)

AC-130 Spectre Gunship

The AC-130 gunship is an airborne gun platform with a howitzer, Gatling guns, and cannons. This provides considerable fire support for ground missions. This aircraft provides close air support for ground troops and air interdiction of enemy forces and supplies. Spectres fly in a constant bank to one side to allow their weapons to fire.

A recent modification allows the gunships to receive video from Predator UAVs, and developmental laptop software, called Rover, allows ground troops to designate hostile and friendly forces right on the video screen. This is then uplinked to the Spectre gunship, resulting in more accurate fire and reducing "friendly fire" incidents.

A laser weapon system is being developed to supplement the array of weapons on the Spectre.

AC-130 Spectre Gunship

US Air Force

General Characteristics

Primary function: Close air support, air interdiction, and force protection
Builder: Lockheed/Boeing Corp.
Power plant: Four Allison T56-A-15 turboprop engines
Thrust: 4,910 shaft horsepower each engine
Length: 97 feet, 9 inches (29.8 meters)
Height: 38 feet, 6 inches (11.7 meters)
Wingspan: 132 feet, 7 inches (40.4 meters)
Speed: 300 mph (Mach .4 at sea level; 484 km/h)
Range: Approximately 1,300 nautical miles (2,410 kilometers); unlimited with air refueling
Ceiling: 25,000 feet (7,576 meters)
Maximum takeoff weight: 155,000 pounds (69,750 kilograms)
Armament: AC-130H/U: 40mm cannon and 105mm cannon; AC-130U: 25mm gun
Crew: AC-130U—Five officers (pilot, copilot, navigator, fire control officer, electronic warfare officer) and eight enlisted (flight engineer, TV operator, infrared detection set operator, loadmaster, four aerial gunners)

Deployment date: AC-130H, 1972; AC-130U, 1995
Unit cost: AC-130H, $132.4 million; AC-130U, $190 million (fiscal 2001 constant dollars)
Inventory: Active duty: AC-130H, 8; AC-130U, 13; ANG, 0; Reserve, 0
(Source: USAF Fact Sheets online)

MH-53—Pave Low

The Pave Low is a heavily armed helicopter for insertion and extraction or resupply of Special Forces behind enemy lines. These aircraft can travel in all weather conditions and at low levels to escape detection by enemy air defenses.

General Characteristics

Primary function: Long-range infiltration, exfiltration, and resupply of Special Operations forces in day, night, or marginal weather conditions
Builder: Sikorsky
Power plant: Two General Electric T64-GE/100 engines

Pave Low

Robert F. Dorr

Thrust: 4,330 shaft horsepower per engine

Length: 88 feet (28 meters)

Height: 25 feet (7.6 meters)

Rotary diameter: 72 feet (21.9 meters)

Speed: 165 mph (266 km/h) at sea level

Ceiling: 16,000 feet (4,876 meters)

Maximum takeoff weight: 46,000 pounds (20,880 kilograms); Emergency War Plan allows for 50,000 pounds

Range: 600 nautical miles (1,113 kilometers); unlimited with aerial refueling

Armament: Combination of three 7.62mm miniguns or three .50-caliber machine guns

Crew: Officers, two pilots; enlisted, two flight engineers and two aerial gunners

Date deployed: 1981

Unit flyaway costs: $40 million (fiscal 2001 constant dollars)

Air Force inventory: Active force, 13 MH-53J's, 25 MH-53M's; ANG, 0; Reserve, 0

160th SOAR

The 160th Special Operations Aviation Regiment, the "Night Stalkers," supports Special Forces with air transport. They fly MH-6 and AH-6 "Little Bird" helicopters for infiltration and extraction of Special Forces. MH-60 and AH-60 are larger helicopters, which have .50-caliber and 7.62mm machine guns, 70mm rockets, Hellfire missiles, night-vision equipment, 30mm cannon and Stinger missiles for air-to-air combat. The MH-47E Chinook is a large twin-rotor helicopter for larger force insertion and extraction and is armed with twin 7.62mm miniguns that can fire up to 6,000 rounds a minute.

Communications

Special Forces as well as CIA paramilitary units use portable satellite terminals to communicate directly with their parent commands, or in the case of the CIA, headquarters at Langley, Virginia.

LST-5C

Typical of the lightweight satellite terminals is the LST-5C made by Motorola. Setup is easy. Knowing latitude and longitude from a GPS receiver, or from map coordinates, the Special Forces operator consults a manual to tell him where to point the antenna for the satellite he wants to use. He points the antenna, turns on the terminal, and moves the antenna back and forth to maximize the satellite signal. At that point he's ready to start contacting other satellite terminals with a view to the same satellite.

He can type messages into his computer, or talk in real time to another terminal. The messages can be encrypted or in the clear.

General Characteristics

Model number: LST-5C

Volume: 209 cubic inches (3,417 cubic centimeters)

Weight: 8.4 pounds (3.8 kilograms)

Antenna: Trivec Avant, Inc.

Capability: wideband voice or data, narrowband data, or digitized voice conference call

Computer: GRID

Transmitter output: 18 watts maximum

Frequency range: 225 to 400 megahertz

Battery type: lithium

Manufacturer: Motorola

(Source: Motorola data sheet)

PRC-112 Squad Radio

Designed for communication with downed pilots, this radio has all the features needed for troops operating behind enemy lines. The transmissions are performed in short bursts to foil any direction-finding attempts by enemy forces.

With the Hook survival radio integrated with the PRC radio, accurate location via GPS is possible to aid in extraction of Special Forces. The GPS capability is the civilian service only, not the military or precision service, to avoid having military crypto-graphic equipment and operational keys fall into enemy hands.

(Source: Federation of American Scientists, www. fas.org)

AN/PSN-11 Precision Lightweight GPS Receiver (PLGR)

This receiver processes signals from several simultaneous Global Positioning satellites to determine the receiver's location, accurate to less than one meter. During the Persian Gulf War, the entire constellation of GPS satellites was not yet deployed, resulting in dropouts of GPS coverage. Many parents of Allied soldiers bought commercial receivers and sent them to their sons and daughters in the Gulf. This time, ground units will be given militarized GPS receivers with advanced antijam and antispoofing capability. GPS transmits a precision code to determine location very accurately. This code is encrypted to prevent the enemy forces from using the most accurate signal available. GPS also transmits a civilian code, which is unencrypted and which has significantly less accuracy. The PLGR is relatively heavy at almost three pounds. It will be replaced in the future by the Defense Advanced GPS Receiver (DAGR).

(Source: "Strong Men Armed: The Marine Corps 1st Force Recon Company" by Pat Rogers in The Accurate Rifle, *May 2001, Volume 4, Number 4)*

Laser Target Designators

Special Forces employ laser target designators to "light up" a target with laser light. The reflected laser light is detected by aircraft overflying the target area, then a bomb is released, which then flies toward the laser light. Accurate strikes with laser-guided bombs are the result, thus avoiding civilian casualties and using the ordnance where it was intended. However, as with any complicated system,

some bombs go astray due to human error, or mechanical or electrical failure.

AN/PAQ-3 Modular Universal Laser Equipment (MULE)

The MULE is a portable laser target designator able to be carried by one man. It is set up on a tripod, or can be shoulder operated. The MULE is able to track moving targets and send range, azimuth, and elevation to a fire control center via an electronic message. The MULE can also be used as a range finder on a moving target up to almost two miles (3,000 meters) away, or a stationary target up to three miles (5,000 meters) away.

One drawback is its very heavy weight and large size. With its night sight, the MULE is over one hundred pounds, severely limiting what its human carrier could carry in addition to the MULE. Given that most attacks in the modern U.S. military are at night, this is a significant limitation. In spite of this limitation, this equipment was successful in the Persian Gulf War and elsewhere.

General Characteristics

Primary function: Target locator and guide for laser-guided projectiles
Manufacturer: Hughes Aircraft
Weight: 42 pounds (19 kilograms) daylight ops; 108 pounds (49 kilograms) with night sight
Laser designator/range finder
Field of view: 4°
Magnification: 10x
Stabilized tracking module
Field of rotation: 360°
Elevation: 16.9° up; 22.5° down
Terrain capability: 0° to 15°
Range: 1.9 miles (3 kilometers), moving target; 3.1 miles (5 kilometers), stationary target
Run time: 10 minutes
Recharge time: 7 hours
Unit replacement cost: $218,000
(Source: USMC Fact File)

AN/PEQ-1A Special Operations Forces Laser Marker (SOFLAM)

The SOFLAM is a more advanced laser target designator than the earlier, quickly deployed MULE. It is much lighter in weight, smaller, and much easier to transport. With its companion, image-intensified night sight, AN/PVS-13, it is capable of day or night operation. The sight will allow the operator to point exactly at the target, which the MULE could not do.

General Characteristics

Primary function: Target locator and guide for laser-guided projectiles
Weight: 12 pounds (5.5 kilograms) daylight ops; 34 pounds (15.4 kilograms) with night sight, AN/PVS-13
Magnification: 10×
Range: 3.1 miles (5 kilometers) target designation; 6.2 miles (10 kilometers) ranging
AN/PVS-13 Night Sight
Sight magnification: 6×
Sight weight: 4.2 pounds (1.9 kilograms)
Sight run time: 40 hours
(Source: "Strong Men Armed: The Marine Corps 1ˢᵗ Force Recon Company" by Pat Rogers in The Accurate Rifle, *May 2001, Volume 4, Number 4)*

U.S. Army Special Forces (Airborne)—Green Berets

The U.S. Army Special Forces, commonly called Green Berets, derive from a World War II unit officially named the First Special Services Force, nicknamed the Devils Brigade, which was a combined Canadian-American unit. This group was trained in explosives, climbing, skiing, amphibious assault, and parachute training. They served in Italy, Alaska, and France. The unit took so many casualties during the war that it was disbanded in 1945.

In 1952 the U.S. Army activated Special Forces under the name U.S. Army Psychological Warfare Division and School, and the unit went through many name changes but stayed at Fort Bragg. Green Berets served with distinction in the Vietnam War; they have the motto *"De Oppresso Liber,"* to free the oppressed.

Modern-day U.S. Army Special Forces train in intelligence, operations, weapons, communications, medicine, and engineering. They also are expected to learn the host country's language to fulfill their mission and to aid and advise forces in-country. All of this requires exceptional intelligence and extreme toughness.

In the field USA SF(A) wear anything but a green beret. They adopt native dress and try to blend in to the countryside while they go about their dangerous missions. Pictures from the war in Afghanistan show these forces with beards and in various dress suited to their need for a low profile. The 5th Special Forces Group were the ones who rode into battle on horseback with anti-Taliban forces during a battle in Afghanistan.

Headquartered at Fort Bragg, North Carolina, USA SF(A) are organized into seven Special Forces Groups, each of which is tailored to a different area of responsibility. The 5th Special Forces Group (Airborne) headquartered at Fort Campbell, Kentucky, is responsible for action against Iraq.

In any future confrontation with Iraq, USA SF(A) will be called upon to aid, train, and advise the forces in Iraq arrayed against Saddam Hussein's regime, the Kurds premier among them. They will also be used for reconnaissance deep behind enemy lines, capturing enemy prisoners, and sabotage of enemy installations.

U.S. Army SF(A) Weapons

The Green Berets intensively train with a variety of weapons, including obsolete weapons that third world countries have in their arsenals. Training school for a weapons specialty is twenty-four months and includes many of the U.S. Army's small arms, mortars, antiair weapons, and antiarmor weapons. To fulfill its training missions in foreign countries, Green Berets become experts in all kinds of tactics and American and foreign weapons as well.

U.S. Army Rangers

The Rangers had their beginnings prior to the American Revolutionary War, when British General Edward Braddock formed several companies of Rangers with the idea of having them take the point for his main army to prevent surprise attack. Robert Rogers took command of the Rangers during the French and Indian War. Colonel Francis Marion led Rangers against the British during the Revolutionary War, sweeping through the South attacking the British and their American supporters, returning each local government to the American side.

During the Civil War, the Ranger name came into disrepute because of a lack of discipline and their preying on the civilian population. Other units, such as Mosby's Rangers and Grierson's Rangers, had better reputations and were effective fighting units. One of Grierson's raids into Mississippi was the subject of a Hollywood movie, *The Horse Soldiers.*

World War II saw the birth of the modern Rangers with a unit begun in 1942 and commanded by Colonel William O. Darby. They were also the subject of a Hollywood movie, *Darby's Rangers.* Inspired by British commandos, the U.S. Rangers trained for the toughest missions over the toughest ground. On D day, June 6, 1944, during the invasion of Normandy, Rangers attacked Pointe du Hoc, fought their way up steep cliffs, and captured German emplacements. The large artillery they were looking for had been moved, but the Rangers had established an important milestone in their history.

In the Far East, Rangers under the command of General Frank Merrill, Merrill's Marauders, attacked the Japanese throughout Burma under the most deplorable conditions, rife with disease and malnutrition.

At the end of World War II, Ranger units were disbanded, then reinstituted for the Korean War. They were again disbanded after the cease-fire in Korea. In 1969 Long Range Reconnaissance Patrols were redesignated Ranger battalions for use in the Vietnam War. Their mission hadn't changed much since before the Revolutionary War: reconnaissance, penetrating deep behind enemy lines, sabotage of enemy supply lines, designation of targets, all the while remaining a highly mobile, supremely capable force, slashing at the enemy rear.

During Desert Storm, Rangers were true to their charter. They moved deep into enemy territory, scouting Iraqi positions and giving intelligence on Iraqi movements and types of equipment. With no place to hide in the desert, they moved underground, digging in and expertly camouflaging themselves. Iraqi soldiers came within ten feet of some Rangers without detecting their presence.

For any upcoming confrontation with Iraq, Rangers would be used as before for behind-the-lines reconnaissance, attacking special targets, and assisting local insurgents against Saddam Hussein. Rangers will be sent into northern Iraq to train, advise, and assist the Kurds.

Rangers used to wear distinctive black berets, but when the rest of the U.S. Army started to wear them over Ranger protests, the Rangers switched to tan-colored berets to stand out from the rest of the U.S. military.

Ranger Weapons

The basic assault rifle of the Rangers is the M16, which is used throughout the U.S. military. M60 tripod-mounted, belt-fed machine guns provide infantry with automatic-weapons fire support. For heavier targets Rangers use an M67 90mm recoilless rifle to take out bunkers, buildings, and armored vehicles. They also employ Claymore mines, named for a legendary Scottish sword, which have 700 steel ball bearings mounted on a shape charge to spray an area with flying metal, lethal up to 160 feet (50 meters). The clacker or detonator can be set off by a trip wire or remotely to attack an enemy troop formation.

True to their Special Forces nature, Rangers own the night and use many different kinds of night-vision equipment from goggles to night weapons sights.

1st SFOD—Delta

The Delta Force is the U.S. elite counterterrorist force. Delta's genesis came in 1963 when a U.S. Special Forces officer named Charlie Beckwith traveled to Malaya with Britain's Special Air Service for missions into the deep jungle against insurgents along the Thai border. Beckwith survived the tour with the SAS and started lobbying to include SAS training with the U.S. Special Forces. The 1st Special Forces Operational Detachment–Delta was born in 1977.

The name Delta is derived from the manner in which Special Forces are organized. Six Alpha teams commanded by captains are in a Bravo detachment. A Bravo team is a company-sized unit commanded by a major. A Charlie team is a battalion commanded by a lieutenant colonel. Because the new unit was organized differently, similar to the SAS, and was commanded by a full colonel, it was assigned the next letter in the alphabet, D, the phonetic designation of which is Delta.

Their first famous mission was the attempt to rescue hostages in Iran in 1980. The mission ended in failure due to mechanical breakdown of two navy helicopters in the Iranian desert. As they departed their desert base, a helicopter crashed into a transport plane and both were destroyed. Several U.S. servicemen were killed. After a thorough review, Delta emerged and has since supported operations in Panama and Grenada, and in the Persian Gulf War they hunted SCUD launchers in the Iraqi desert.

Delta Weapons

Delta weaponry is greatly varied and is tailored to the mission at hand. For close-quarters combat, perhaps in a house or a building, the Heckler Koch MP5 machine gun is used for its prodigious firepower and small size. For covert missions Delta may use an HK MP5 with an integral silencer. Close-quarters combat may dictate the use of shotguns, the Mossburg 12 gauge being the weapon of choice. M16s are used for the more traditional military missions, many with an integral grenade M9 Beretta 9mm launcher attached to the underside.

Two types of handguns are used, the M1911A1 .45-caliber automatic, which has been around since 1911, and the newer 9mm Beretta Model 92 FS, to which most of the U.S. military has switched.

For sniping rifles the 7.62mm M40A1 Remington and the 7.65mm M21 Springfield, which is similar to the M14, are used.

Modern grenades come in the form of a soup can and can be frag grenades, concussion, or the flash-bang grenades invented by the British SAS. They can be thrown by hand or launched in a grenade launcher.

SEALs

SEAL stands for Sea Air Land, which are the different points from which a U.S. Navy SEAL can attack an enemy. They wade ashore like marines, drop from the sky on parachutes like airborne, or attack at sea with quick seizure and close-in combat techniques. The SEALs have their beginnings with the underwater demolition teams, UDT, of World War II. At Tarawa the marines were offloaded 500 yards offshore when the landing craft got hung up on coral, only to die by the hundreds under the withering fire from the Japanese defenders. The need was clear from this disaster for a force to go in before the battle and blow up underwater and beach obstacles, clearing lanes for landing craft. UDTs did just that in many battles in the Pacific.

UDT teams (called Navy Combat Demolition Teams, NCDTs) also cleared beaches at Normandy, suffering 40 percent casualties. In Korea at Inchon, the site of a brilliant invasion by U.S. forces that resulted in a North Korean rout, they also cleared lanes of mines the old-fashioned way, one mine at a time.

SEALs were commissioned in 1962, serving in Vietnam by advising the Vietnamese navy, taking on special missions behind enemy lines, and ranging up and down the Mekong Delta ambushing enemy patrols, taking prisoners for intelligence interrogation, and targeting enemy formations.

Navy SEALs can exit from a submarine or from a DDS (a Dry Deck Shelter attached to the deck of a submarine), join up in an SDV (Swimmer Delivery Vehicle), and come ashore at night. SEALs also can be driven ashore by the Special Boat Squadrons, SBS. The SBS operate in shallow coastal areas, and as such they are called the Brown Water Navy. Whichever way the SEALs come ashore, they will be on the enemy before the enemy knows what's happening.

SEAL Weapons

SEALs use many of the same weapons in service elsewhere in the U.S. military. M16s, or the CAR-15, a shorter version with a collapsible stock that enables users to get in and out of cramped spaces, are used as the main weapons. Many of these weapons have an M203 grenade launcher under the barrel. The Heckler Koch MP5 is also used. One version of the MP5 is a small machine gun with virtually no barrel extending beyond the front hand grip. Called the room broom, it is used in very-close-quarters combat, and as the name implies, it is used to sweep a room of the enemy.

The M60 belt-fed machine gun used by the SEALs is a stripped-down lightweight version, tolerant of sand, which eventually gets into everything a SEAL has. Claymore mines are used for enemy ambushes and for rear-guard protection as a SEAL squad moves through enemy territory.

For sniping, SEALs use Haskins .50-caliber rifles for targets within a mile and a half. For harder targets, like an armored personnel carrier, or APC, the Barrett 82A1 uses armor-piercing or incendiary

ammunition out to over a mile (1,800 meters). This weapon is so effective that it can take the place of a mortar or rocket crew. M67 round throwing grenades are used, and the 40mm grenade is launched by the M203 described previously.

For concealment, a Special Forces imperative, SEALs wear "ghillie" suits handmade by the men during their training. They are a mesh weave, net-type fabric with strips of brown and green cloth woven haphazardly through the top portion to conceal a trooper's head as he sets up in hiding to recon or snipe at the enemy.

U.S. Marines Force Recon

At Camp Pendelton in 1954 the Force Recon was born when an organization was needed to test methods of insertion of forces into enemy territory for reconnaissance purposes. The 1st Force Reconnaissance Company was formed a few years later in 1957.

In Vietnam, Force Recon conducted 2,200 reconnaissance patrols and sadly left forty-four men missing or killed in action.

Force Recon mission profiles are divided into two types: direct action and deep reconnaissance. Direct action includes sea platform and ship boarding, search and seizure, capturing of enemy personnel behind enemy lines, and recovery of aircraft and personnel in rescue situations. Deep reconnaissance includes identification of enemy formations, location, weapons, vehicles and armor, terrain surveillance, laser designation of targets for guided munitions, and poststrike evaluation. Other duties can be personnel security for selected individuals in a theater of war.

Force Recon can be inserted into enemy territory in various ways via air, ground, or sea. They use some of the same insertion equipment as the Navy SEALs and other U.S. Special Forces. They can rappel from helicopters, hit the beach using submersible equipment, or parachute in various ways, for example HALO (high altitude, low opening) from 35,000 feet up.

Force Recon Weapons

Marine Force Recon members use the M16, as many other Special Forces do, but are switching to the M4A1 for close-quarters combat with a collapsible stock and an attachable silencer, or more accurately, a noise suppressor. No shot is ever completely silenced. The M4 can also hold an M203 grenade launcher under the barrel, and can mount a lithium-battery-operated optical sight. A night-vision sight is also available and a laser pointer to aid in aiming can be mounted. Colt Commandos, or CAR-15s, are also in use with Force Recon.

For pistols, Force Recon uses the M1911 .45-caliber automatic, the M9 Beretta 9mm automatic with 15-round magazines, and curiously the small-caliber High Standard HD, which fires a .22-size long-rifle round and has a silencer. This weapon has its origins in the OSS during World War II. It is used for relatively quiet shots at close range. Also for close-quarters work, Force Recon uses Mossberg and Remington 12-gauge riot shotguns.

For rapid fire to pin down large numbers of enemy troops, Force Recon relies on the SAW, Squad Automatic Weapon, a 200-round magazine-fed machine gun, and the M240, a gas-operated, belt-fed machine gun.

Snipers in Force Recon use the M40A1 rifle and the M80A3 .50-caliber rifle, which also have day optical sights and night-vision sights.

Special Air Service (SAS), U.K.

Britain's Special Air Service is the model upon which many counterterrorist and Special Forces are based throughout the world. Their motto is "Who Dares Wins." This group of legendary Special Forces is notoriously secretive about their activities. Their ranks come from the regular army, who then undergo grueling physical and mental training to test their capabilities. The SAS was born in World War II, when they were deemed so dangerous that the Germans were ordered to shoot them on sight. They caught the public's attention when they cleared the Iranian embassy in London of terrorists, and again during the war with Argentina over control of the Falkland Islands.

Although strictly enjoined to keep SAS activities secret, many books have been published by former members, providing a glimpse into this very secret, elite force. The SAS activities in northwest Iraq during the Persian Gulf War were detailed in *Bravo Two Zero* by Andy McNab.

The SAS consists of three regiments, the 22nd SAS Regiment, and the 21st and 23rd SAS Regiments. The 22nd gets all the attention because they are the ones who go into combat. The other two are TA, Territorial Army, regiments, or reserve units. Each regiment is made up of four Sabre Squadrons. Four troops make up a Sabre Squadron, each troop specializing in a distinct area. The troops are designated Air Troop, Boat Troop, Mobility Troop, and Mountain Troop. Troops have sixteen men in each, and are rotated for cross-training purposes so that each man has detailed knowledge of at least two different specialties.

SAS Weapons

The SAS primarily uses the M16, often with an under-the-barrel grenade launcher attached. Heckler Koch MP5s are used for close-in combat, as might be needed in clearing a building of enemy troops. The standard rifle for the British army is the SA80, but this is not used by the SAS unless they are disguised as regular army troops. For sniper duties the SAS uses the Barrett Model 82A1, a .50-caliber weapon. Handguns used are the SIG-Sauer P226, or the easily concealable Walther PPK.

Claymore mines are also used by the SAS against enemy troops, and the 66 shoulder-launched rocket is used against buildings and light armor.

Sensors—Satellites

During the Persian Gulf War, six or seven imaging satellites were in operation. All these satellites made two passes over the Gulf region every day; thus every two to four hours a U.S. satellite was imaging the area, providing both wide-area and narrowly focused images. These images were correlated to determine Iraqi armor, artillery, and personnel movements, as well as battle damage assessments. Imagery was relayed to the United States and to reception facilities in the Gulf region, allowing Allied commanders near-real-time imagery intelligence. Some selected imagery is provided to field commanders using portable, low-data-rate receivers, which enable field forces to see the enemy's positions in front of them.

KH-11 Imaging Spacecraft

Three of these spacecraft provided optical images with a resolution of approximately six inches during the Persian Gulf War. These spacecraft also have high-resolution capabilities for detecting objects at night. This constellation of satellites has fixed orbits that cover the earth's entire surface every few days. Because of this, adversaries can predict when one is overhead and conceal targets until the satellite passes by.

Advanced KH-11 Imaging Spacecraft

Two or three of this version of the venerable series of imaging satellites were in service during the Persian Gulf War. To avoid the "fixed orbit" limitation, these satellites were designed to be maneuverable, making it extremely difficult to predict when one is overhead. Instead of coming over a target at a fixed angle, their maneuverability allows many angles, making photos from its advanced sensors much more valuable in characterizing targets and assessing battle damage.

Lacrosse

This satellite's main sensor is a synthetic aperture radar, SAR. This type of radar is used on a moving platform to extend the size of its aperture, or antenna view, to create high-resolution images through complex signal processing. Originally deployed to detect Warsaw Pact armor in Europe, this satellite easily detects Iraqi armor in the desert.

During the Persian Gulf War, Iraq's mobile SCUD launchers were tracked by correlating radar images from Lacrosse and optical images from the KH-11 series satellites. In contrast with the KH satellites, Lacrosse can image targets through cloud cover and at night.

DSP—Defense Support Program Spacecraft

Two of these spacecraft provided infrared views of the battlefield during the Persian Gulf War. This enabled Pentagon planners to see a SCUD launch in real time and warn surrounding allies that a missile was on its way. These satellites have twelve-foot infrared telescopes with 6,000 infrared detectors each. DSPs are in geosynchronous orbits and as a result are over the region continuously, effectively almost "staring" at the battlefield. The telescopes are offset at an angle, and the entire spacecraft is rotated slowly so that the telescope view sweeps over the region every few seconds. This allows a narrower field of view and higher image resolution.

The detailed resolution of these satellites allowed afterburner plumes from fighters over the Persian Gulf to be observed during the Persian Gulf War.

KH-12 (Improved Crystal)

This satellite has optical sensors that operate in visible, near-infrared and thermal-infrared bands that have enhanced ability to detect camouflaged and buried structures by comparing temperature differences. These differences can be used to determine whether factories are being used, along with determining recent use of aircraft and vehicles, especially tanks and armor. Its image resolution is up to 10 centimeters (2.5 inches).

Improved Crystal has increased fuel for enhanced maneuverability to avoid having predictable orbits with static arrival-over-target times.

KH-13

This is an improved stealth version of KH-12 in that it is undetectable by radar or infrared sensors to protect against antisatellite weapons. It has electro-optical infrared sensors.

8X

This is a very large multifunction satellite with enhanced optics in Molniya orbits, which are elliptical in nature, allowing longer view times over target areas. The advantage is that it has an adjustable dwell capability, which is very useful for tactical battlefield situations. A multisatellite constellation is projected, which would have a satellite passing over any spot on earth every fifteen minutes. Fuel tanks are very large, refuelable by the Space Shuttle, which give 8X a significant maneuvering capability.

Sensors—Aircraft

E-3 Sentry—AWACS

The E-3 Sentry is an airborne warning and control system (AWACS) aircraft with a radar in a rotating dome over its fuselage. The radar is very sophisticated, with a range of 250 miles. Its ability to separate out aircraft from ground radar returns, called clutter, is highly developed. Air traffic controllers are part of the crew, and they provide air management over a region. AWACS provides all-weather surveillance, command, control and communications needed by U.S. and Allied commanders.

General Characteristics

Primary function: Airborne surveillance, command, control and communications
Primary sensor: Radar
Builder: Boeing Aerospace Co.
Power plant: Four Pratt & Whitney TF33-PW-100A turbofan engines

E-3 Sentry

US Air Force

Thrust: 21,000 pounds each engine
Length: 145 feet, 6 inches (44 meters)
Wingspan: 130 feet, 10 inches (39.7 meters)
Height: 41 feet, 4 inches (12.5 meters)
Rotodome: 30 feet in diameter (9.1 meters), 6 feet thick (1.8 meters), mounted 11 feet (3.33 meters) above fuselage
Speed: Optimum cruise 360 mph (Mach 0.48; 580 km/h)
Ceiling: Above 29,000 feet (8,788 meters)
Maximum takeoff weight: 347,000 pounds (156,150 kilograms)
Endurance: More than 8 hours (unrefueled)
Unit cost: 123.4 million (fiscal 1998 constant dollars)
Crew: Flight crew of four plus mission crew of 13 to 19 specialists (mission crew size varies according to mission)
Date deployed: March 1977
Inventory: Active force, 33; Guard, 0; Reserve, 0
(Source: USAF Fact Sheets online)

E-8C Joint Surveillance Target Attack Radar System—JSTARS

During the Persian Gulf War, JSTARS was in development, but engineers installed its sophisticated electronics into two aging Boeing 707 airframes in time to significantly contribute to the war effort. Its radar provided images of the battlefield and located Iraqi formations, tanks, vehicles, and artillery, which gave a near-real-time picture of the battlefield to coalition field commanders.

General Characteristics

Primary function: Airborne battle management
Primary sensor: Radar
Primary contractor: Northrop Grumman Corp.
Power plant: Four Pratt & Whitney TF33-102C engines
Thrust: 19,200 pounds each engine
Length: 152 feet, 11 inches (46.6 meters)

E-8 Joint Stars

US Air Force

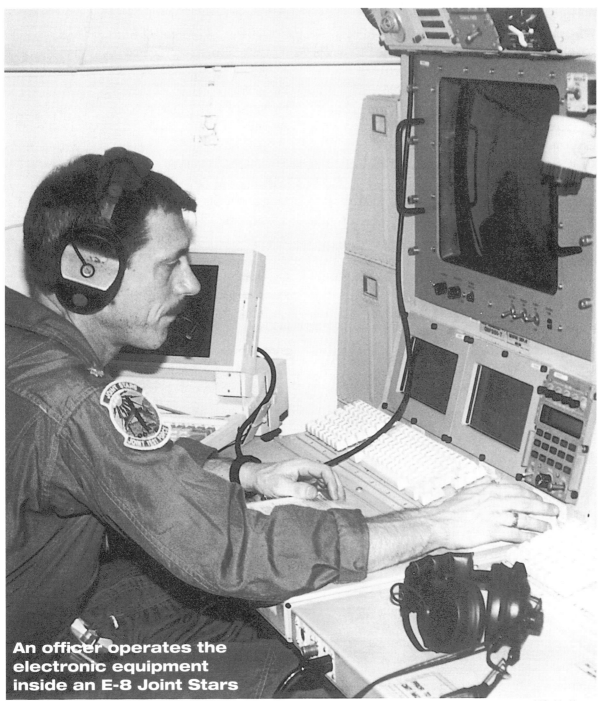

An officer operates the electronic equipment inside an E-8 Joint Stars

US Air Force

Height: 42 feet, 6 inches (13 meters)

Wingspan: 145 feet, 9 inches (44.4 meters)

Speed: Optimum orbit speed 390–510 knots (Mach 0.52–0.65; 723–946 km/h)

Ceiling: 42,000 feet (12,800 meters)

Maximum takeoff weight: 336,000 pounds (152,410 kilograms)

Endurance: 9 hours (unrefueled)

Unit cost: $244.4 million (fiscal 1998 constant dollars)

Crew: Flight crew of four plus fifteen Air Force and three Army specialists (crew size varies according to mission)

Date deployed: 1996

Inventory: Active force, 13 (16 to be delivered by 2004); ANG, 0; Reserve, 0

(Sources: USAF Fact Sheets online, and Triumph Without Victory *by the* U.S. News & World Report *Staff, Random House, 1992)*

UAVs—RQ-1 Predator

The RQ-1 Predator is an unmanned air vehicle (UAV) that features long endurance and two main sensors, a color camera, and a synthetic aperture radar for ground surveillance and target acquisition. The Predator is armed with Hellfire missiles and can take out enemy armor, hardened bunkers, or any enemy installation in the field.

General Characteristics

Primary function: Airborne surveillance, reconnaissance, and target acquisition

Primary sensor: Color nose camera and synthetic aperture radar

Armament: Hellfire antitank missile

Contractor: General Atomics Aeronautical Systems Incorporated

Power plant: Rotax 914 four-cylinder engine producing 101 horsepower

Length: 27 feet (8.22 meters)

Height: 6.9 feet (2.1 meters)

Weight: 1,130 pounds (512 kilograms) empty; maximum takeoff weight is 2,250 pounds (1,020 kilograms)

Wingspan: 48.7 feet (14.8 meters)

Speed: Cruise speed around 84 mph (70 knots; 135 km/h), up to 135 mph (218 km/h)

Range: up to 400 nautical miles (454 miles; 732 kilometers)

Ceiling: up to 25,000 feet (7,620 meters)

Fuel capacity: 665 pounds (302 kilograms; 100 gallons)

Payload: 450 pounds (204 kilograms)

System cost: $40 million (1997 dollars)

Inventory: Active force, 48; ANG, 0; Reserve, 0

(Source: USAF Fact Sheets online)

UAVs—Global Hawk

The Global Hawk unmanned aerial vehicle (UAV) differs from the Predator in that it flies at very high altitudes, surveying large areas and providing battlefield commanders near-real-time, high-resolution surveillance and reconnaissance imagery. Another difference is that the Global Hawk is unarmed. Global Hawk provides imagery via its optical, infrared, and synthetic aperture radar sensors.

This UAV flies autonomously based on preprogrammed inputs and sends data back to battlefield commanders via satellite relay or ground stations. Global Hawk can survey 40,000 nautical square miles in just one day.

Global Hawk

US Air Force

General Characteristics

Primary function: Airborne surveillance, reconnaissance, and target acquisition

Primary sensors: synthetic aperture radar, optical and infrared sensors

Armament: none

Contractor: Northrop Grumman

Length: 44 feet (13.4 meters)

Weight: 25,600 pounds (11,612 kilograms) fully fueled

Wingspan: 116 feet (35.3 meters)

Speed: 340 knots (about 400 mph; 645 km/h) for 35 hours

Range: 12,000 nautical miles (22,258 kilometers)

Ceiling: 65,000 feet (19,812 meters)

(Source: USAF Fact Sheets online)

U-2

This venerable aircraft has been in use since the 1950s and became notorious when pilot Gary Powers was shot down on a U-2 mission over the Soviet Union during the Eisenhower administration. The U-2 provides continuous, high-altitude, all-weather surveillance and reconnaissance in direct support of U.S. and Allied intelligence agencies, ground, and air forces.

General Characteristics

Primary function: High-altitude reconnaissance

Primary sensors: multisensor photo, electro-optic, infrared, and radar

Contractor: Lockheed Martin Aeronautics

Power plant: One General Electric F-118-101 engine

Thrust: 17,000 pounds

Length: 63 feet (19.2 meters)

Height: 16 feet (4.8 meters)

Wingspan: 105 feet (32 meters)

Speed: 475-plus mph (Mach 0.58; 766-plus km/h)

U-2

Department of Defense

Maximum takeoff weight: 40,000 pounds (18,000 kilograms)

Range: 7,000 miles (6,090-plus nautical miles; 11,290 kilometers)

Ceiling: Above 70,000 feet (21,212-plus meters)

Crew: One (two in trainer models)

Date deployed: U-2, August 1955; U-2R, 1967; U-2S, October 1994

Cost: Classified

Inventory: Active force, 37 (four two-seat trainers and two operated by NASA); ANG, 0; Reserve, 0

E-2C Hawkeye

The E-2C Hawkeye is the U.S. Navy's all-weather, carrier-based tactical warning and control system aircraft. Each carrier carries two of these aircraft, and they are kept flying most of the time when out to sea. They form a carrier battle group's eyes and ears on what is happening over the horizon, where a ship's radar cannot reach.

General Characteristics

Primary function: Airborne early warning, command and control

Primary sensor: Radar

Contractor: Grumman Aerospace Corp.

Propulsion: Two Allison T-56-A427 turboprop engines (5,000 shaft horsepower each)

Length: 57 feet, 6 inches (17.5 meters)

Wingspan: 80 feet, 7 inches (28 meters)

Height: 18 feet, 3 inches (5.6 meters)

Weight: Maximum gross takeoff: 53,000 pounds (23,850 kilograms); 40,200 pounds basic (18,090 kilograms)

Speed: 300-plus knots (345 mph; 552 km/h)

Ceiling: 30,000 feet (9,100 meters)

Crew: Five

Armament: None

Unit cost: $51 million

Operational: January 1964

E-2C Hawkeye

US Navy

Sensors—National Security Agency Sensors

NSA has listening posts around the globe, picking up electromagnetic signals from any transmitter in a target area. These passive listening stations relay information back to NSA headquarters in Fort Meade, Maryland, where encrypting codes are broken and messages analyzed using state-of-the-art supercomputers.

NSA also has listening assets in orbit, which pick up many electromagnetic signals from terrestrial sources of interest. One satellite, Magnum, has seen some publicity. Designed to replace lost listening ground stations when the Iranian revolution overthrew the Shah, this satellite is believed to have an enormous antenna in order to receive terrestrial signals on orbit. One is said to have been positioned in geosynchronous orbit (stationary with respect to the Earth) at a point where it could receive signals from Russian line-of-sight microwave stations. The low-level signals are amplified and sent down to NSA Earth stations for analysis.

Iraqi Forces

State of the Iraqi Military

Before the Persian Gulf War the Iraqi armed forces totaled over 900,000 men in forty-seven divisions. After Desert Storm, the ground war in the Gulf, the Iraqi military dropped to about 350,000 men in twenty-four divisions with 2,300 tanks and 1,000 artillery pieces. This is not to say that the difference in personnel numbers were all casualties; the coalition Allies did not kill, wound, or capture almost 600,000 men. Estimates are that Iraq suffered perhaps 10,000 dead and 63,000 captured. The rest were probably released from duty and returned to civilian life. The International Institute for Strategic Studies estimated in mid-2002 that Iraq had 375,000 men in seventeen divisions with 2,500 tanks and 1,900 artillery pieces. It is evident that Saddam Hussein has increased his army and tried to reequip it slowly in spite of sanctions imposed by the United Nations, though not with much success.

The Iraqi army's most effective forces remain the Republican Guard, and though during the Persian Gulf War they were the only units to put up any kind of effective fight, they were outmaneuvered and outgunned by U.S. and U.K. armored divisions and pounded from the air by coalition air forces. They currently number approximately 80,000 men in six divisions and are the most capable of the Iraqi land forces. However, in any war with Iraq the U.S. and its allies will not let the Republican Guard come into play or inflict any substantial casualties on Allied forces. The Allies have the knowledge, experience, and capability to keep the Republican Guard at arm's length until air power has decimated their ranks. In any land battle, the results can be expected to be the same as in the Persian Gulf War—the Guard will be outmaneuvered and outgunned by superior tactics, equipment, and tank crews.

The Special Republican Guard of about 16,000 resides in Baghdad, acting as Saddam's security force. Any Allied units wanting to capture Saddam Hussein himself would have to go through these dedicated forces, although they cannot be expected to withstand a determined assault from superior Allied forces.

The Iraqi air force was devastated during the Persian Gulf War, losing more than 500 aircraft, including most of its fighters, 34 to coalition air power and the rest when they were sent to Iran, never to return. Current estimates total 130 attack aircraft, and 180 fighters plus support aircraft. Possibly 90 or so are able to carry out missions. The only new hardware introduced into the Iraqi air force since the Persian Gulf War is an air-to-air missile, the Matra Magic, with a range of only 8 miles (12.9 kilometers) or so. With the U.S. AMRAAM air-to-air missile, which has a range of greater than 20 miles (32 kilometers) and the U.S. Navy's Phoenix missile's maximum range of 100 miles (160 kilometers), the Iraqi pilots will not stand much of a chance against U.S. pilots.

There has been some reconstitution to Iraq's air defenses in the last decade. But with ground-to-air combat occurring almost every day in the no-fly zones and with Iraq coming out on the short end in every encounter, it is evident that the Iraqi air defense system is no match for the highly trained Allied pilots and their highly sophisticated aircraft.

The Iraqi navy was almost completely destroyed during the Persian Gulf War. Their only contribution to Iraqi defense was the sea mines, which struck some U.S. ships in the Persian Gulf. Iraq possesses five batteries of Chinese Silkworm antiship missiles, but the Allied navies will stay out of range of these missiles until they are destroyed by aircraft or cruise missiles. Strategically the Iraqi navy meant nothing to the war effort during the Persian Gulf War, and they will mean nothing in any upcoming confrontation.

Estimates of current (late 2002) forces and equipment in the Iraqi military:

Total personnel: 389,000
Reserves: 650,000

Army

Total personnel: 350,000 (including 100,000 recalled reservists)
Composed of:
    7 Corps HQs
    3 armored divisions
    3 mechanized divisions
    11 infantry divisions
    6 Republican Guard divisions
    4 Special Republican Guard brigades
    5 Commando brigades
    2 Special Forces brigades
Equipment
Main battle tanks: 2,600 total
    1,900 T-55/62 and PRC Type-59
    700 T-72

Recon vehicles: 400
    Brdm-2, AML-60/90
    EE-9 Cascavel
    EE-3 Jararaca
Armored infantry fighting vehicles: 1,200
    BMP 1/2
Armored personnel carriers: 1,800
    BTR 50/60/152
    OT 62/64
    MTLB
    YW-701
    M-113A1/A2
    EE-11 Urutu
Towed artillery: 1,900
    105mm (including M-56 pack)
    122mm (including D-74, D-30, M-1938)
    130mm (including M-46, Type 59-1)
    155mm (including G-5, GHN-45, M-114)
Self-propelled artillery: 200
    122mm (2SI)
    152mm (2S3)
    155mm (including M-109A1/A2, AUF-1 [GCT])
Multiple rocket launchers: 200
    107mm
    122mm (BM-21)
    127mm (ASTROS II)
    132mm (BM-13/16)
    262mm (Ababeel-100)
Mortars: (numbers unknown)
    81mm
    120mm
    160mm (M-1943)
    240mm
Surface-to-surface missiles
Launchers reported:
    50 Free Rocket Over Ground (FROG)
    6 SCUD (possibly possess Al Hussein also)
Antitank guided weapons: (numbers unknown)
    AT-3 Sagger (including BRDM-2)
    AT-4 Spigot
    SS-11
    Milan
    High-subsonic Optically Teleguided (HOT)—includes 100 VC-TH

Recoilless launchers: (numbers unknown)
  73mm (SPG-9)
  82mm (B-10)
  107mm (B-11)
Antitank guns: (numbers unknown)
  85mm
  100mm (towed)
Helicopters: 164
Attack: 62
  12 Mi-25
  20 SA-319
  10 SA-316
  20 SA-342
Support: 102
  20 SA-330-F
  30 BO-105
  10 Mi-6
  30 Mi-8
  12 Mi-17
Surveillance equipment: (numbers unknown)
  RASIT (Armored Reconnaissance Radar—detects vehicles and artillery)
  Cymbeline (antimortar radar)

Navy

Total personnel: 2,000
Patrol and coastal combat vessels: 6
Missile craft: 1 Soviet Osa I Fast Patrol Craft with 4 SS-N-2A Styx surface-to-surface missiles
Inshore patrol craft: 5 (all believed inoperable)
  1 Soviet Bogomol Fast Patrol Craft (inshore)
  1 other Fast Patrol Craft (inshore)
  1 Patrol Craft (inshore)
  80 boats
Mine warfare craft: 3
Mine countermeasures:
  1 Soviet Yevgenya
  2 Nestin minesweepers (inshore)
Support and miscellaneous:
  1 Damen miscellaneous auxiliary vessel
  1 yacht (with helicopter deck)

Air Force

Total personnel: 20,000
Total combat aircraft: 316 (no armed helicopters)
Aircraft
Bombers: 6
  H-6D
  Tu-22
Fighter, ground attack: 130
  MiG-23BN
  Mirage F1EQ5
  Su-20
  40 Su-22 M
  2 Su-24 MK
  2 Su-25
Fighter: 180
  18 F-7
  40 MiG-21
  50 MiG-23
  12 MiG-25
  50 Mirage F-1EQ
  10 MiG-29
Reconnaissance: 5 MiG-25
Tanker: (numbers unknown)
  Includes: 2 Il-76
Transport: (numbers unknown)
  An-2
  3 An-12
  An-24
  6 An-26
  Il-76
Training: (numbers unknown)
  20 AS-202
  50 EMB-312
  50 L-39
  Mirage F-1BQ
  25 PC-7
  12 PC-9
Missiles
Air-to-surface include: Am-39, AS-4, AS-5, AS-9, AS-11, AS-12, AS-30L, C-601
Air-to-air include:
  AA-2/6/7/8/10, R-530, R-550

Air Defense Command

Total personnel: 17,000
Headquarters: Baghdad/Al Muthanna
Regional air defense centers:
Kirkuk (north)
Kut al Hayy (east)
Al Basrah (south)
Ramadia (west)
Air defense guns: 3,000
23mm: ZSU-23-4 SP
37mm: M-1939 and twin
57mm: include ZSU-57-2 (self-propelled)
85mm
100mm
130mm
Surface-to-air missiles: Approximately 850
launchers
Includes SA-2/3/6/7/8/9/12/13/16, Roland, and
Aspide

Paramilitary forces
Total personnel: 42,000–44,000
Security troops: 15,000
Border guards: 9,000
Saddam's Fedayeen: 18,000–20,000

Iraqi Air Power

MiG-21—NATO Code Name: Fishbed

The MiG-21 is a Soviet delta-wing aircraft exported to many countries allied with the Communist bloc. It is used in air-to-air combat, reconnaissance, electronic countermeasures, and ground attack. Some MiG-21s are configured with two seats for training. It is considered a good dogfighter in the hands of a competent pilot against most contemporary Western aircraft.

MIG-21

US Air Force

General Characteristics

Crew: One pilot, or two pilots (operational trainers)

Maximum speed: Mach 2.1 at high altitude

Maximum range: 683 miles (1,100 kilometers)

Combined radius: 400 nautical miles (742 kilometers) with two 550-pound (250-kilogram) bombs

Armament (main): One twin-barrel 23mm GSh-23 gun and two to four AA-2 Atoll missiles

Weight: 11,465 pounds (5,200 kilograms) without weapons

Country of manufacture: Russia

In service: 40

(Source: Center for Defense Information online)

MiG-23—NATO Code Name: Flogger

The MiG-23 is another of the Soviet aircraft set up for export to allied nations. It has swing-wing design and is used for intercept missions and fighter roles. It can also serve as a ground-attack aircraft (MiG-23BN). The MiG-23's speed, Mach 2.35, is comparable to many Western fighters, and in the hands of a competent pilot the aircraft can present problems to Allied air forces. The MiG-23 also has an indentification-friend-or-foe capability (IFF) and an advanced missile system.

General Characteristics

Crew: One pilot

Maximum speed: Mach 2.35 (at height 72-degree sweep)

Maximum range: 1,210 miles (1,950 kilometers)

Combined radius: 715 miles (1,150 kilometers) with six air-to-air missiles

Armament (main): 1 23mm gun in fuselage belly pack

Weight: 22,485 pounds (10,200 kilograms)

Country of manufacture: Russia

In service: 50

MIG-23

US Navy

MiG-25—NATO Code Name: Foxbat

This very high speed aircraft caused much concern on the part of Western militaries when it was first introduced decades ago. When a Soviet pilot defected to Japan with a MiG-25, U.S. intelligence agencies swarmed over it. What they found was a very heavy *steel* fuselage, which was beginning to rust. Analyzing weight and engine fuel efficiency, intelligence discovered that the combat radius was very short, severely limiting its effectiveness as a fighter-interceptor. Furthermore, the radar, while very powerful, was built with *vacuum tubes*. The combination of a steel fuselage (most modern aircraft are made of aluminum or titanium for lightness and strength) and a vacuum-tube radar showed a very primitive design, causing intel sources to ridicule the MiG-25.

The snickering was cut short, however, when the intel teams got back to Washington and the spin doctors took control of the media coverage. The emphasis was placed on the high-powered radar, which could burn its way through jamming, and the high speed (near Mach 3), which would cause a host of troubles for Western aircraft. It may have been developed to intercept the U.S. SR-71, a Mach 3 reconnaissance aircraft.

The MiG-25 operates in all weather conditions, day and night, and in dense, hostile electronic warfare environments (high-power radar would defeat this). It has a nose-mounted fire control radar and infrared search track sensor. Its air-

MIG-25

US Navy

frame was designed for high speed, not maneuverability, which makes it ineffective as a dogfighter. It has an identification-friend-or-foe (IFF) capability and an advanced missile system.

General Characteristics

Crew: One pilot, or two pilots (operational trainers)

Maximum speed: Mach 2.83–3 at high altitude

Maximum range: 1,075 miles (1,730 kilometers)

Combined radius: 900 miles (1,450 kilometers)

Armament (main): air-to-air missiles, AA-6 "Acrid" under each wing

Weight: Nearly 44,100 pounds (20,000 kilograms)

Country of manufacture: Russia

In service: 12

MiG-29—NATO Code Name: Fulcrum

This fighter is probably the most capable of all the Soviet aircraft exported to allied nations and is certainly the best fighter/attack aircraft in the Iraqi arsenal. The MiG-29 has all-weather, day and night capability in an active or passive jamming environment. Its maneuverability and weapons systems are of great concern to Allied air forces, but with only ten aircraft in the Iraqi inventory, Allied forces should be able to take these aircraft out early in the war. The MiG-29 is armed with R-27R1 medium-range missiles with radar homing heads, and unguided weapons for hitting ground and sea-surface targets.

General Characteristics

Crew: One pilot

Maximum speed: Mach 2.35

MIG-29

US Air Force

Maximum range: 1,305 miles (2,105 kilometers)

Combined radius: 930 miles (1,500 kilometers)

Armament (main): Six R-60MK air-to-air missiles, or four R-60MK and two medium-range R-27R1 and a built-in GSh-301 gun (30mm caliber)

Weight: 24,030 pounds (10,900 kilograms)

Country of manufacture: Russia

In service: 10

F-7 Fighter Aircraft

This fighter is a day-only-capable aircraft exported by China. Its combat radius is even shorter than the MiG-25 and MiG-23, but on par with the MiG-21. It has a single seat and a single engine, but has air and ground attack capability. It has some Western avionics but is not expected to pose any problems for Allied air forces.

General Characteristics

Crew: One pilot

Maximum speed: Mach 2.35

Maximum range: Ferry range 1,080 miles (1,740 kilometers) with two air-to-air missiles and two 480-liter drop tanks, or 1,380 miles (2,230 kilometers) with three 720-liter drop tanks

Combined radius: 400 miles (650 kilometers), long-range interception with two air-to-air missiles and three 720-liter drop tanks at Mach 1.5

Armament (main): Two 30mm cannons, Type 57-2 air-to-air missiles, one Type 90-1 air-to-ground rocket, and 227-pound (500-kilogram) bombs

F-7

Department of Defense

Weight: Empty: 11,620 pounds (5,275 kilograms); normal takeoff: 16,590 pounds (7,531 kilograms)
Country of manufacture: China
In service: 18

F-1EQ Mirage—Attack/Fighter Aircraft

The Mirage's greatest asset is the large amount of external munitions that can be carried. The Mirage is imported from France and has a sophisticated attack system and all-weather capability, with an Inertial Navigation System, and a naval attack central computer. A CRT heads-up display projects aircraft and weapons status on the windscreen so that the pilot does not have to look downward to access that information.

Its armament is highly capable, boasting air-to-air and antiradiation missiles. Prior to the Persian Gulf War, an Iraqi Mirage launched a French Exocet missile at the USS *Stark,* causing significant damage and killing thirty-seven sailors.

General Characteristics

Crew: One pilot, or two pilots (operational trainers)
Maximum speed: Mach 2.2 at high altitude
Maximum range and combined radius: 265 miles (427 kilometers) in high-low-high mode at Mach 0.75 with fourteen 550-pound (250-kilogram) bombs
Armament (main): Two 30mm DEFA 553 cannon, Matra Super 520 air-to-air missiles, and one Amrat antiradar missile, or one AM39 Exocet antiship missile for ground attack
Weight: 16,314 pounds (7,400 kilograms)
Country of manufacture: France
In service: 50
(Source: Center for Defense Information online)

SU-22 Attack Aircraft—NATO Code Name: Fitter

This older aircraft is imported from the former Soviet Union and features a swing-wing configuration. It was modified many times, emphasizing different missions, including as a low-level bomber and as a trainer. It was designed as a fighter-bomber but was used mostly as a bomber. With a cruising range of over 1,000 miles (1,613 kilometers), the Su-22 is an effective aircraft with capable avionics and impressive armament.

General Characteristics

Similar aircraft: MiG-21 Fishbed, Su-7 Fitter, A-7 Corsair II, G-Y91
Crew: One
Role: ground attack
Length: 61 feet, 6 inches (18.76 meters)
Span: 45 feet (13.8 meters)
Designation: Su-22 Fitter F
Ceiling: 59,000 feet (18,000 meters)
Cruise range: 1,080 miles (1,750 kilometers)
In-flight refueling: No
Internal fuel: 8,700 pounds (3,950 kilograms)
Payload: 7,710 pounds (3,500 kilograms)
Sensors: Terrain-following radar, RWR, ballistic bomb sight
Drop tanks: 800-liter drop tank with 1,400 pounds (639 kilograms) of fuel for 76 nautical miles (141 kilometers)
Armament: Cannon: NR-30 30mm
AS-7, AS-9, AS-10, AA-8 antiair missiles, FAB-500 bombs
Countries of origin: CIS (Commonwealth of Independent States, formerly USSR)
User countries: Afghanistan, Algeria, Iran, Iraq, Libya, North Yemen, Peru, South Yemen, Syria, Vietnam
(Source: Federation of American Scientists, www.fas.org)

SU-22

Robert F. Dorr

SCUD—Al Hussein and Other Surface-to-Surface Missiles

Iraq successfully developed the Al Hussein missile from imported SCUD missiles—it imported 819 SCUDs from the Soviet Union in the 1980s. Iraq then used hundreds of these missiles to attack Iranian cities during the Iran-Iraq War. Iraq then undertook to indigenously produce these missiles. Tehran, some 300 miles (484 kilometers) from the Iran-Iraq border, was outside the range of the unmodified SCUD-B, which can travel a maximum distance of only 186 miles (300 kilometers). To overcome this deficiency, Iraq extended the range of the SCUD twice, apparently relying heavily on foreign technical assistance and equipment.

The first upgrade, called the Al Hussein, had a range of 370 to 400 miles (600 to 650 kilometers), and could attack Tehran during the Iran-Iraq War. Its payload was increased to approximately 660 to 770 pounds (300 to 350 kilograms). The Al Hussein corresponds more or less to the SCUD-B due

to its similar size and would put most of Israel and all of Syria within striking range. Sixty of these missiles were fired at Saudi Arabia and Israel during the Persian Gulf War in January and February of 1991.

Variants include the Al Hussein Short and the Al Hijarah. According to unconfirmed information from October 1990, Iraq was producing missiles for use against oil wells and people. The Al Hijarah missiles are designed to release poison clouds that would kill personnel on the ground and ignite oil wells. The Iraqis claimed to have fired at least one of another SCUD variant, which apparently had a concrete-filled warhead, at Israel during Operation Desert Storm. A total of four or five of these Al Hussein missile variants were probably fired during the Persian Gulf War, including at least one Al Hijarah, which landed in the Negev Desert near the Israeli nuclear facility near Dimona. In addition Iraq admitted deploying seventy-five of its SCUDs with chemical and biological warheads into the field to use against Israel and coalition forces during the Persian Gulf War.

As of 1996 UNSCOM maintained that Iraq was still concealing six to sixteen enhanced SCUD missiles, potentially able to deliver chemical or biological warheads. These Al Hussein missiles eluded UNSCOM inspectors, along with as many as twenty long-range missile warheads produced before 1991 specifically to carry biological weapons. By 1996 UNSCOM concluded that Iraq had produced eighty SCUD-like missiles indigenously.

Other more ominous developments were started by Iraq. A 560-mile (900-kilometer) range missile, called al-Abbas, was based on SCUD technology. A two-stage missile called Badr-2000 was begun and is said to have a range of 465 to 620 miles (750 to 1,000 kilometers).

General Characteristics

Payload weight: 660 to 770 pounds (300 to 350 kilograms)
Payload capability: explosive, chemical, biological warhead
Length: 37 feet (11.2 meters)
Diameter: 3 feet (0.9 meters)
Range: 370 to 400 miles (600 to 650 kilometers)
Variants: Al Hussein Short;
Al Hijarah—chemical warfare
Inventory: UNSCOM estimates 6 to 16
(*Source: Federation of American Scientists, www. fas.org*)

Iraqi Ground Forces

T-72 Battle Tank

This Soviet tank was considered one of the most capable of any armored vehicle in the Eastern bloc. Built low to the ground, it is very hard to target and hit. The U.S. M1A1 tank has thermal sights that normally give the M1 a great advantage; however, the T-72 has its engine and exhaust covered in such a way as to not emit much heat. When dug into the desert floor, the T-72 doesn't present much to look at. The T-72 main gun's range is shorter than the M1A1 by a few hundred meters, but U.S tanks were likely to get well within the T-72's main gun range before the American crews were able to detect its presence. Its main 125mm gun is capable of penetrating the U.S. M1A1's armor at up to 0.6 miles (1,000 meters). It has laser range finders and night-vision equipment. The T-72 is considered tough to beat even with the latest American armor. However, there is a vulnerable spot on the sides just below the turret where an armor-piercing round can enter and destroy it.

General Characteristics

Crew: Three
Combat weight: 44.5 metric tons
Chassis length: 22.7 feet (6.91 meters)
Height: 7.2 feet (2.19 meters)
Width: 11.7 feet (3.58 meters)
Engine type: 840-horsepower diesel
Cruising range: 310–558 miles (500–900 kilometers) with external tanks
Speed: 37 mph (60 km/h) maximum road; 28 mph (45 km/h) maximum off-road
Average cross-country: 22 mph (35 km/h)
Armor, turret front: 520–950mm against HEAT
Applique armor: Side of hull over track skirt, turret top
Explosive reactive armor: Kontakt or Kontakt-5 ERA
Ancillary equipment: Mine-clearing equipment, self-entrenching blade, NBC protection system
Smoke equipment: Smoke grenade launchers (8×81mm left side of turret), and thirty-two grenades. Vehicle engine exhaust smoke system.
Main armament: 125mm smoothbore gun 2A46M/D-81TM

Ammunition: 125mm APFSDS-T, BM-42M

Maximum aimed range: 1.9 miles (3,000 meters)

Maximum effective range: 1.24–1.9 miles (2,000–3,000 meters) day; 0.5–0.8 miles (850–1,300 meters) night

Armor penetration: 590–630mm at 1.24 miles (2,000 meters)

Rate of fire: 4–6 rounds in two minutes in manual mode

Loader type: Autoloader (separate loading) and manual

Ready/Stowed rounds: 22/23

Elevation: –6° to +14°

Range finder: TPD-K1M laser range finder

Fire on move: Yes, up to 15 mph (25 km/h). Depending on the road and distance to the target, most crews may halt before firing.

Auxiliary weapon: 7.62mm (7.62 × 54R) machine gun PKT

Antitank guided missiles: AT-11/SVIR

Warhead type: Shaped charge or tandem shaped charge (HEAT)

Armor penetration: 700–800mm

Range: 2.5 miles (4,000 meters)

Name: AT-11B/INVAR

(Source: Federation of American Scientists, www. fas.org)

RASIT—Armed Reconnaissance Radar

The radar is mounted on a multiwheeled vehicle for traversing rough terrain like that found in the Iraqi desert. It is used to detect artillery for counterbattery fire and to detect vehicles. When the fighting starts, Iraq will be virtually blind from the air with only the hope that these vehicles can do some good.

General Characteristics

Purpose: Detect vehicles and artillery

Engine performance: 320 horsepower

Weight: approximately 16.7 tons (15,164 kilograms)

Maximum speed: approximately 56 mph (90 km/hr)

Operating range: approximately 500 miles (800 kilometers)

Radar coverage: to 12.4 miles (20 kilometers)

Crew: Four

Armament: One Fla MG 7.62mm

(Source: Federation of American Scientists, www. fas.org)

Iraqi Air Defense—Surface-to-Air Missiles

Aspide

The Aspide is an air-to-air and surface-to-air missile based on the U.S. military's Sparrow. The Aspide is manufactured in Italy. It can be launched from both ships and ground platforms. This missile is a semiactive homing weapon, which uses the aircraft, ship, or ground radar to illuminate the target while the missile's radar receives the reflected radar pulses and homes in on the target.

General Characteristics

Manufacturer: Selenia, Italy

Date deployed: 1987

Range: 47 miles (75 kilometers)

Ceiling: 26,240 feet (8 kilometers) above the launch point

Speed: Mach 4 (2,900 mph; 4,680 km/h)

Propulsion: One SNIA-Viscosa solid-propellant rocket motor

Guidance: Selenia monopulse semiactive radar homing

Warhead: 72.75-pound (33-kilogram) SNIA Difesa e Spazio blast fragmentation: Doppler proximity and direct-action fused

Launch weight: 485 pounds (220 kilograms)

Length: 12 feet, 1.67 inches (3.7 meters)

Diameter: 8 inches (203 millimeters)

Fin span: 3 feet, 3.4 inches (1.0 meter)

(Source: Federation of American Scientists, www. fas.org)

Roland II

The Roland weapon system is a surface-to-air missile designed to defend mobile units from air attack. It is effective against aircraft flying up to Mach 1.5 and against hovering helicopters. Roland has a radar with a range of 10 miles (16 kilometers) and is mounted on a tracked vehicle or in a fixed shelter. Roland has an infrared sight, which measures the difference between the missile while in flight and the fire control radar line of sight, and is capable of remote control.

General Characteristics

Range: 3.7 miles (6 kilometers) maximum, 0.5–1.25 miles (0.7–2 kilometers) minimum

Altitude: 3.4 miles (5.5 kilometers)

Basic load on vehicle: 10 missiles (2 per launcher)

Detection range: 10 miles (16.5 kilometers)

Reaction time: 4–10 seconds

Firing time: first shooting: 8–10 seconds; later shooting: 2–6 seconds

Speed: Mach 1.6

Reload time: approximately 10 seconds

Probability of hit: 80 percent

Warhead: HE hollow charge

Command guidance: RF SACLOS or CLOS

Radar(s): Siemens/Thomson-CSF D-band pulse Doppler search radar, Thomson-CSF J-Band monopulse Doppler tracking radar

Setup/Teardown time: 3 minutes

Chassis: AMX-30, Marder APC, trucks, or in fixed shelters

(Source: Federation of American Scientists, www. fas.org)

SA-12A

The SA-12 is a tactical surface-to-air missile system, which also has antiballistic missile capabilities. This SAM system is on a tracked vehicle and can be maneuvered quickly into position. The guidance system is inertial with semiactive radar homing.

General Characteristics

Range: 3.7–47 miles (6–75 kilometers)

Altitude: 82,000 feet (25 kilometers)

Basic load on vehicle: 4 missiles on launcher

Speed: 1 mile per second (1.7 kilometers per second)

Warhead: 330-pound (150-kilogram) HE

Command guidance: Combined, inertial with semiactive self-guidance

Radar(s): Grill Pan missile guidance radar, Bill Board surveillance radar, High Screen sector scan radar

Setup/Teardown time: 5 minutes

Support vehicles: TELAR, Transloader, command post

Chassis: Variations of the MT-T chassis are used for the launch vehicle, loader-launcher vehicle, missile guidance station, command post vehicle, and the radars.

SA-13

The SA-13 is a short-range, low-altitude SAM system. The SA-13 is designed to defend ground troops from low-level air strikes by aircraft and helicopters, cruise missiles, air-to-surface missiles, RPVs, and UAVs. The SA-13 has a dual-mode guidance system for the missile seeker—optical and passive IR. The SA-13 also has identification-friend-or-foe capability (IFF).

General Characteristics

Total length: 7.2 feet (2.2 meters)
Diameter: 4.7 inches (0.12 meters)
Wingspan: 15.75 inches (0.4 meters)
Weight: 92 pounds (42 kilograms)
Warhead: 11-pound (5-kilogram) HE
Maximum speed: Mach 2
Effective range: 0.4–3.1 miles (600–5,000 meters)
Altitude: 33–11,500 feet (10–3,500 meters)
Guidance mode: IR homing, cooled seeker, dual frequency
Basic load on vehicle: 8 missiles
Reload time: 3 minutes
Fire control: IR homing, cooled seeker, dual frequency
Radar(s): Snap Shot (range only); Pie Rack (IFF)
Setup/Teardown time: 40 seconds
Support vehicles: 14631
Chassis: MT-LB
Speed: 37 mph (60 km/h) road; 3.7 mph (6 km/h) water
Crew: Three
(*Source: Federation of American Scientists, www. fas.org*)

SA-16

SA-16 is a surface-to-air missile system capable of being carried by troops in the field. The SA-16's missile has an infrared guidance system using an improved two-color seeker, likely infrared and ultraviolet (UV), which is designed to detect the difference between flare decoys and an aircraft's jet engine.

General Characteristics

Maximum speed: Mach 2-plus
Effective altitude: 11,500 feet (3,500 meters)

Effective range: 0.3–3.1 miles (500–5,000 meters)
Altitude: 33–11,500 feet (10–3,500 meters)
Warhead: 4.4-pound (2-kilogram) HE
Guidance: passive two-color IR and UV homing
Fuse: Contact and graze
(*Source: Federation of American Scientists, www. fas.org*)

New Iraqi Weapons Since the Persian Gulf War

Matra Magic

The R550 Magic 1 and 2 is an air-to-air missile that is guided by an infrared, nitrogen-cooled seeker in the missile's nose. The Magic 2 has a Doppler fuse and has semiactive radar homing, which means the target is illuminated by the aircraft's radar and the radar returns are received by the missile. Its chief drawback is the very short range, just over 8 miles (12.9 kilometers). It is powered by a solid-propellant motor and armed with a fragmentation warhead.

If used in a war against allies led by the United States, this weapon will not be very useful. Allied aircraft will engage Iraqi aircraft at much greater distances and not allow Iraqi aircraft to get within range.

General Characteristics

Major operational capabilities: All-directions missile
Builder: Matra
Propellant: Solid propellant
Propulsion time: 2.2 seconds
Range: 8 miles (12.9 kilometers)
Speed: Mach 2.7
Length and diameter: 2.75 meters by 0.16 meters
Weight: 196 pounds (89 kilograms)
Warhead: HE blast fragmentation

Payload: 27.5 pounds (12.5 kilograms) fragmentation

Guidance: All-aspect infrared

Fuse: Radio frequency (RF) proximity

In service in the French air force: 1988

Main user nations: Greece, Egypt, Spain, Kuwait, United Arab Emirates

Possible carrying aircraft: All French air force and navy fighters

(Source: The Federation of American Scientists, www.fas.org)

Mine Warfare

Iraq made extensive use of mines during the Persian Gulf War. The land mines formed barriers across southern Iraq on its border with Saudi Arabia and throughout Kuwait, along its coast and on some offshore islands. The Iraqi military did this in anticipation of not only a land invasion from Saudi Arabia, but also an invasion from the Persian Gulf by U.S. Marines. One might imagine how the Iraqi commanders relished the prospect of an invasion into the built-up defenses around Kuwait City. The Iraqi strategy was to inflict massive casualties on the coalition forces and have the American people demand a premature end to the war. However, the seaborne marines in the Gulf were used as a feint to draw Iraqi troops away from the Saudi Arabian border, and the spectacle of marines throwing themselves on barbed wire and taking casualties in extensive minefields never happened. However, 34 percent of the casualties in the coalition forces were due to mines.

Land Mines

Iraq's land mines come from various countries and are equipped with pressure, trip wire, and magnetic fuses. Iraqi minelayers placed their mines with rigid precision across the battlefield during the Persian Gulf War. They put antitank mines four to five meters apart with antipersonnel mines one meter from the antitank mines. This sort of regularity played against the Iraqis as the coalition forces quickly caught on and used the pattern to locate and destroy the land mines.

MK154 Mine-Clearance Launcher

This system is used to clear a lane through a minefield during an amphibious assault and subsequent operations inland. The MK154 LMC, mounted in an AAVP7A1, can deploy three linear demolition charges on water or land. Each linear demolition charge (LDC) is over 300 feet (100 meters) long. The charge is only effective against single impulse, non-blast-resistant, pressure-fused mines. Because of this, another mechanical device must also be used in the same area to ensure that all mines have been cleared.

General Characteristics

Primary function: Land mine clearance system

Manufacturer: Diesel Division, General Motors of Canada, Ltd.

Host vehicle: Assault Amphibious Vehicle (AAVP7A1)

Weight: 3,040 pounds (1,368 kilograms); with shipping container: 8,790 pounds (3,991 kilograms); fully loaded: 10,690 pounds (4,853 kilograms) (includes three linear demolition charges and three rockets)

Vehicle height (with MK154 installed): 127.95 inches (3.25 meters)

Inventory: 75

Unit replacement cost: $155,000

(Sources: U.S. Marine Corps Fact Files and Maxwell Air Force Base)

M1 Mine-Clearing Blade System

The M1A1 Main Battle Tank can be fitted with a mine-clearing blade system to take land mines out of a lane of travel. It is capable of clearing mines down to a depth of six feet in the tank's path.

General Characteristics

Primary function: To effectively counteract and neutralize all land mines

Manufacturer: Israel Military Industries

Weight: 4.5 tons (4.1 metric tons)

Length: 9.6 feet (2.9 meters)

Width: 14.9 feet (4.5 meters)

Height: 2.5 feet (2.3 meters)

Square: 143 square feet (13.3 square meters)

Cube: 346 cubic feet (10.4 cubic meters)

Inventory: 71

(Source: U.S. Marine Corps Fact Files)

Sea Mines

Iraq also used sea mines and had several fields barring the Kuwaiti coast. These mines were of three types: moored, floating, and influence mines. Moored mines are exactly what the name implies: mines fixed to the sea bottom via a tether. Floating mines do exactly that; they free-float and explode when near a large piece of metal, such as a ship, or they explode on contact. These first two types of mines are the easiest to detect. Influence mines are most likely moored directly to the seabed with-

out the use of a tether, and can be very difficult to detect. Influence mines listen for the sound of a ship passing over and also detect the magnetic signature of passing ships. When the right signals are received, the mine explodes.

Two U.S. warships were hit by mines, USS *Tripoli* (LPH-10) and USS *Princeton* (CG-59), with seven casualties total. USS *Tripoli*, the flagship in one of the most extensive minesweeping operations since the Korean War, sustained a sixteen-by-twenty-foot hole in the forward starboard side below the waterline when it hit a moored or floating mine. The resulting explosion caused minor flooding to six auxiliary spaces, and was minimized by damage control procedures. Four crew members were injured, and the amphibious assault ship remained fully mission capable. USS *Princeton* hit two influence mines, sustaining damage including a crack in her superstructure, a jammed port rudder, and a leaking port shaft seal. It then got under way on half power. Three crewmen were injured, one seriously.

Mine Detection

AN/PSS-12 Metallic Mine Detector

This mine detector is a handheld device and is waved over the ground by troops as they advance through a suspected minefield.

General Characteristics

Primary function: Mine detection

Manufacturer: Schiebel Instruments, Inc.

Power supply: Four 1.5-volt batteries

Operating time: 70 hours

Weight: 8.5 pounds (3.8 kilograms); in transport case, 13.7 pounds (6.2 kilograms)

Deployment method: Handheld

Materials: The telescopic pole consists of an inner plastic tube and outer aluminum tube.

Unit replacement cost: $1,196

USS *Raven* (MHC 61)— Mine Hunter, Coastal

The USS *Raven* is one of the Osprey-class of mine-hunting ships. These ships use sonar and video systems, cable cutters, and a mine-detonating device that can be released and detonated by remote control. They are also capable of conventional sweeping measures. The ships' hulls are made of glass-reinforced plastic (GRP) fiberglass to lower their magnetic signature and avoid detonating a magnetic mine.

General Characteristics

Overall length: 188 feet (57 meters)
Extreme beam: 38 feet (11.6 meters)
Maximum navigational draft: 11 feet (3.4 meters)
Full displacement: 904 tons
Dead weight: 87 tons
Hull material: Composite hull
Number of propellers: Two
Propulsion type: Diesel engines
Crew: Officers, five; enlisted, forty-six
(Source: The USS Raven *Web page)*

Advanced Mine Detection

ALISS, Advanced Lightweight Influence Sweep System, can safely detonate acoustic and magnetic sea mines in shallow water. It uses a superconducting coil to form a very powerful magnetic field to imitate the magnetic signature of a ship. Coupled with a sound maker, this system tricks influence mines into thinking that a ship is passing overhead. The mine then explodes harmlessly. ALISS can also be operated by remote control on an unmanned vessel entering minefields without endangering any naval personnel.

The Magic Lantern Deployment Contingency System is the development program looking into laser detection of mines. The lead development program within this overall program is the Airborne Laser Mine Detection System (ALMDS) to detect floating and keel-depth moored mines. Laser mine detection was demonstrated in 1995. This system will detect and identify mines in shallow water and in surf to be cleared for landing craft operations. This capability is going to be incorporated into the U.S. Navy's LAMPS antisubmarine helicopters and on UAVs in the future.

Source Material

Two sources in particular have been used extensively to research this book. These are:

Federation of American Scientists, www.fas.org, and
Center for Defense Information online, www.cdi.org

The military Web sites have also been particularly helpful:

USAF Fact Sheets, www.af.mil
U.S. Navy Fact Sheets, www.navy.mil
U.S. Marine Corps Fact File, www.usmc.mil

The Central Intelligence Agency report "Iraq's Weapons of Mass Destruction Programs," October 2002, provided a valuable overview of Iraq's efforts in this critical area.

An outstanding, highly detailed article by Pat Rogers, "Strong Men Armed: The Marine Corps 1st Force Recon Company," in *The Accurate Rifle,* May 2001, Volume 4, Number 4, provided much information on the U.S. Recon Marines. Not much detail is available on this secretive organization except in this article.

Glossary

AAA Antiaircraft Artillery

ANG Air National Guard

APC Armored Personnel Carrier

AGM Air-Guided Missile

AMRAAM Advanced Medium-Range Air-to-Air Missile

APFSDS Armor-Piercing, Fin-Stabilized Discarding Sabot round for antiarmor battles

BLU Bomb Live Unit

CALCM Conventional Air-Launched Cruise Missile

Calutron This is used to separate uranium isotopes to purify U-235, which can be used in a nuclear bomb

CBU Cluster Bomb Unit

CLOS Command Line of Sight

DDS Dry Deck Shelter, an enclosure attached to the deck of a submarine containing SEALs, who exit the shelter and perform underwater missions

DSMAC Digital Scene Matching And Correlation for cruise missiles

DWFK Deep Water Fording Kit for use on a tank

EMP Electromagnetic Pulse created by a nuclear detonation at altitudes of 100 to 200 miles or by specialized high-tech equipment on a UAV. This would couple into anything that can carry an electrical current and create huge currents, thus burning out many electrical devices throughout the country or over a designated target area.

EXOCET French sea-skimming air-to-surface missile. One launched by an Iraqi aircraft struck the USS *Stark,* killing thirty-seven sailors in a pre–Persian Gulf War incident.

GBU Guided Bomb Unit

GPS see **Navstar**

HARM High-Speed Antiradiation Missile

HE High Explosive

HEAT High-Explosive Antitank antiarmor round

HEDP High-Explosive, Dual-Purpose antiarmor round

HESH High-Explosive Squash Head antiarmor round

HMMWV High-Mobility Multipurpose Wheeled Vehicle, nicknamed the Humvee

HPM High-Powered Microwave

IFF Identification, Friend or Foe. A transponder system used on aircraft and missiles that responds to a radio inquiry whether it is "ours" or "theirs."

INS Inertial Navigation System

IR InfraRed, or heat. The portion of the electromagnetic spectrum below visible light in frequency. Infrared is used in targeting for some missiles and "smart" bombs.

JASSM Joint Air-to-Surface Standoff Missile

JDAM Joint Direct Attack Munition

JSOW Joint Standoff Weapon

Mach Mach 1 denotes the speed of sound; Mach 2, twice the speed of sound, etc. Named for Ernst Mach, an Austrian physicist, who pioneered the study of shock waves.

MOPP Mission-Oriented Protective Posture

MTI Moving Target Indication, the capability of a radar to detect moving targets in the presence of a large ground return signal

NATO North Atlantic Treaty Organization

NBC Nuclear, Chemical, and Biological

Navstar Navigation System using Timing And Ranging; the Global Positioning System, GPS, is a constellation of twenty-four satellites that send out navigation signals. Users with the proper receivers can locate themselves with an accuracy of less than one meter. Many modern munitions guidance systems include GPS receivers to aid in finding the proper location for detonation.

NCDT Navy Combat Demolition Team, the name for UDT teams during World War II

OBC Optical Bar Camera, used on the SR-71; it produces long-range panoramic pictures with a resolution of twelve inches

OSS Office of Strategic Services, in existence during World War II, the forerunner of the CIA

RF Radio Frequency

RPV Remotely Piloted Vehicle

RSO Reconnaissance Systems Officer, the backseater in an SR-71 who controls a variety of sensors

SACLOS Semiautomatic Command Line of Sight

SAM Surface-to-Air Missile

SAR Synthetic Aperture Radar, a radar whose motion on a moving platform is used to extend the size of its antenna, or aperture, by the use of signal processing. Very high resolution of targets is the result. These radars are used on aircraft and satellites to obtain detailed information of the earth or a specific target.

SEAL Sea, Air, Land, the U.S. Navy's elite Special Forces

SFW Sensor-Fused Weapon

SLAM Standoff Land Attack Missile; Harpoon air-to-surface antiship missile

SLAM-ER Standoff Land Attack Missile Expanded Response

SMAW Shoulder-launched multipurpose Assault Weapon

TERCOM Terrain Contour Mapping for Tomahawk cruise missiles

TERPROM TERrain PROfile Matching

TMD Tactical Munitions Dispenser

TOW Tube-launched Optically-tracked Wire-guided missile for attacking tanks and other armored vehicles and hardened bunkers

UAV/UCAV Unmanned Air Vehicle/Unmanned Combat Air Vehicle

UDT Underwater Demolition Team

UV Ultraviolet, that portion of the electromagnetic spectrum above visible light in frequency

WMD Weapons of Mass Destruction; nuclear, chemical, and biological weapons capable of inflicting mass casualties

WSO Weapons Systems Officer

About the Authors

John T. Campbell is a communications systems engineer with over thirty years' experience working in the aerospace industry. He served in the U.S. Navy, attaining the rank of lieutenant, and sailed around the world aboard the USS *Shangri-La,* CVA-38. His military experience served as the background for his first published novel, *Raid on Truman*, a fictional account of an attempt to hijack a nuclear aircraft carrier. *Raid* became a national bestseller. John's experience in the aerospace industry led to two other novels, *COBRA DANE* and *Sub Zero,* which were published soon thereafter. *Raid on Truman* and *Sub Zero* have also been published in Japan.

His latest novel is *Vauclain's Shield,* a thriller about an engineer who invents a perfect missile defense system, then realizes that nuclear horror can come from many different sources, even from within the United States itself.

John is a graduate of Villanova University and received a master's degree from the University of Pennsylvania.

He lives in Pennsylvania with his wife and family.

John's Web site is http://members.tripod.com/tekauthor/home.html.

Christine Townsend has worked as an engineer for a large defense company. She has experience in the satellite industry as well as the telecommunications industry. She is a graduate of Villanova University, where she obtained a bachelor's degree in electrical engineering and a master's of science in electrical engineering. She now lives in Phoenixville, Pennsylvania, with her husband.

John and Christine are father and daughter.